WAKE UP

How to Live a Healthy Vibrant Lifestyle

Edited by
Steven E Schmitt

FIRST EDITION

Wake Up Inc
California

CONTENTS

Text in Minion Pro, Helvetica Neue, and Raleway.

First Edition, 2018, manufactured in USA
1 2 3 4 5 6 7 8 9 10 LSI 23 22 21 20 19 18

All stories, photographs, and author biographical details, in this edition, are reproduced by kind permission of the authors.

ISBN-13: 978-0-9994978-1-4 (Paperback)

Additional copies and bulk purchases can be made by contacting:

Steven E Schmitt
Wake Up Inc
PO Box 4251,
Westminster, CA, 92684

www.bestsellerguru.com

Disclaimer:

This Book contains information by various authors that is intended as help and general advice on wellness and health issues. Always consult your doctor for your individual needs. Before beginning any new exercise program it is recommended that you seek medical advice from your personal physician. Any story in this Anthology is not intended to be a substitute for the medical advice of a licensed physician. Wake Up Inc, does not accept any liability as a consequence of following directions or instructions or advice contained in these stories. The reader should consult with their doctor in any matters relating to his/her health.

INTRODUCTION

"How to Live a Healthy Vibrant Lifestyle"

Welcome to *Wake Up: How to Live a Healthy Vibrant Lifestyle* [2018], a collection of authors specifically conceived and designed to give you, the reader, as wide a range of unique perspectives on living a healthy vibrant lifestyle as possible. So if you are reading this book, it is meant to be.

Essentially this is a practical workbook about how to become healthy in body and mind, from thought leaders in their individual fields from around the globe, offering unique perspective on how best to achieve that goal. We believe it will provide a comprehensive insight into attaining and maintaining a vibrant and healthy lifestyle. In fact, I guarantee that there is literally something for everyone, from healthy eating and physical training, to financial health in retirement.

Each author, at the end of his or her story, has a personal biography with contact information. We encourage you to take full advantage of this opportunity to reach out to any author of your choice for further information and personal coaching.

I would like to take this opportunity to thank my fellow authors for the excellent work they have doing all over the world. It is genuinely awe inspiring to see the writing of so many health conscious people gathered in one place to share their unique messages, secrets, and stories.

I would like to thank in particular, Jason Christoff, who was kind enough to pass on to me a number of thought provoking and meaningful quotes. I share them with you, as you read through the wonderful stories in this Anthology:

> *"Whatever you like doing, you can do it better, and do it longer, when you're healthy."*

"As we heal ourselves, we heal the world."

"You don't have to know exactly how live, just know that whole, organic food makes you healthy. Just stick it in your mouth and start the healing process."

"Every cellular compound used to build, repair, and maintain your body, can be found in natural, whole, organic food."

"Out with the old, in with the true."

"Don't end up being the person with the nicest car in the hospital parking lot or the richest person in the grave yard."

"Health is wealth. Everything else is short sighted, short term planning."

"Why do hospitals contain soda, chocolate bar, and snack machines? Why does your doctor never review your dietary habits? Why does your doctor only get paid when you're sick and not when you're healthy? Ask simple questions in order to get the most simple and the most powerful answers."

While you are reading this book, keep in mind that your body has the power to heal and restore itself to ultimate health. A healthy body first starts with a healthy mind and spirit. I sincerely wish you true health, happiness, and prosperity.

Steven E Schmitt,
Laguna Beach, CA, 2018

WAKE UP

How to Live a Healthy Vibrant Lifestyle

Living Every Moment From the Heart

Coco Luo

Imagine, growing up in a very small village in one of the poorest areas in China. The wooden cottage that I grew up in was hand-built by my father and it had no running water or electricity. My parents were uneducated subsistence farmers growing their own food and raising livestock, such as pigs, chickens, geese, and ducks to be sold at the local market to make a living. This also paid the fees for schooling for my sister, my brother, and me.

Life was hard on the farm. My parents worked 14 to 18 hour days every day, plus my sister, brother, and me had to help on the farm as well to make ends meet.

While growing up, nature was our playground. I was a very curious little girl and had thousands of questions with no one to answer them. I remembered watching my mom cook, make our clothes, wash our clothes and hanging the clothes on the clothesline to dry. My mother told me, "You have to watch me because someday you will have to do all these chores for yourself." I knew inside, deep down within me, that this was not the life that I wanted! I do not know how I knew it, other than that deep inner feeling called intuition that made me believe that this way of life was not for me. From early on, I developed a strong inner conviction that I was destined for a whole different way of life where I could leave a positive imprint upon the universe in my own unique way and change the world for the better. I had no idea how, I just knew I needed to do it?

I took it upon myself from an early age to explore the world around me and somehow get some of my questions answered. I knew from this moment on that I needed to see more of what was out there in the world and get out of the limiting environment I was in. After high school, I left for the big city. I looked for work and landed over ten jobs in two years and got fired from five of them. Something in me was unhappy with that style of work-culture. It took away my independence, creativity and freedom of expression and led me to leave China to explore new opportunities in America.

Four years ago, I left China with limited resources on a business trip to various locations in the United States. I had very little money and no friends. A client, who I did business with, was very kind and helped me to find a place to stay, and I started to learn how to live in the United States. It was very hard at first, it took a while for me to get used to life here. I was very sad and lonely at first, but I did not allow this short-term suffering and fear of the unknown to hold me back. I was here with a dream and no one but me would be responsible for the life choices I made. I had to be strong and move forward and listen to my inner convictions. Even though it was very challenging in the beginning, I had to figure out everything by myself through trial and error.

I started to open myself up and quickly found friends and new business opportunities. It was then that a friend of mine took me to a Yoga class. I deeply connected and embraced Yoga as a way of life. That's exactly what I needed at that time, a place where I belonged, I could really feel like I was at home. I started opening up to learning how to live a heart-centered life and began my Yoga teacher training, so that I could share the joy of being and the happiness I felt with others through teaching Yoga.

In the past few years, I have met many people and came across many clients who I found out were not happy or satisfied with their current situation. I was really shocked, living in the wealthiest country in the world, how come the happiness ratio is so low? When I was little, we did not have a lot, but we were really happy. That made me start to do a lot of research and to work even closer with my clients to find out the root cause of all this negativity and suffering. I felt obligated to do everything I can to help everyone around me to bring back the happiness and joy in their life, to live with purpose, and to help them reach their own highest potential in life.

I had always known that Yoga was an ancient healing science but I became fascinated with the idea that a heart-centered practice could heal the world. Yoga is a spiritual practice. One of my main goals of studying and practicing Yoga is to raise the energy level of my spiritual self and the energy of those around me. To me, Yoga is a way of life focused and lived from the heart. My belief is the value of that calm state that allows me to move actions and behaviors from the head to the heart. Practicing Yoga cultivates and develops heart-intelligence that fills up the heart with positive influences and experiences.

The reason why so many people struggle to find lasting happiness and get stuck in their life is because they fall into the "I'll be happy when" syndrome. The only way to find fulfilment is to shift the focus to right now, right this moment. Be calm and live in the present.

Listed below are five ways to improve life and increase lasting happiness:

- Find Freedom from illusion.
- Feel Connection with something greater.
- Discover your Passion for creativity.
- Bring Clarity to your life.
- Live life from the heart and Love one another.

Freedom:

You are not alone if you feel trapped, stuck or afraid to make changes in your life. While we may speak about freedom, what does it really mean to you? Or, how would it feel to be free from the constraints that we and society place upon ourselves? What would life be like if we had freedom from the fear of guilt and worry, and could create the life we know we deserve? Where would you go, where would you live, if you could go anywhere or do anything you wanted without limitation? Free yourself from the chains that bind.

Connection:

Many people share the concept that connection is the most powerful community experience they have had in their lives; when they connect with others in a deep and authentic way; when they feel accepted as who they are; and when they are able to share themselves with others. This opens up the opportunity to be your best self. To be the self you are, and not the self that others want you to be.

Clarity:

When you have clarity about who you are, what is important to you, and what you want out of life, many previously challenging decisions become easy to make: The path that you need to take in order to live a meaningful and purposeful life will become clear. This is the power of clarity. Clear your mind of all negative thoughts and feel the tranquility that it brings.

Passion:

Life can be challenging if you are not passionate about where you are going, especially when things get in your way. Instead of going over, through or around life's obstacles, you may instead just stand still or change direction entirely, but don't give up. Passion is the fuel that keeps us going and makes us unstoppable. Do what you love and love what you do. If you don't have it yet, find your passion!

Live and Love:

You get to choose your way of life, whatever that may be. What you think, believe and act upon will mold your life. If you have filled your life with baggage from the past, wipe it clean.

Erase everything from your past that does not serve you. And, be grateful it brought you to this place now, to a new beginning. You can have a clean slate now, you can start over this very moment, the present is all there is. Find your purpose and live your life fully with joy and tranquility, and fulfill your highest potential with love. Remember, today is the first day of the rest of your life. Make every moment count.

About the Author

Coco Luo

I am a work in progress. I take courses, seminars and workshops to enhance my growth that keeps me present, grounded, and vibrant. A few words that define me are: Freedom, Action, Happiness, Health, Wealth, Wellness, Courage, Love, and Passion. I love sharing my passion of life with others and to help them grow physically, mentally, emotionally, and spiritually. Let us develop a heart-centered practice that will shine through the darkness. I know life is a reflection of what happens inside us and I love helping people explore their inner journey of change and transformation; like the metamorphosis of a caterpillar into a butterfly. Live your life to the fullest with freedom, connection, clarity, passion, and love from your heart.

Connect with Coco Luo (Heath, Wealth & Wellness Coach). I love being in touch with my readers. Here is how to connect with me:

1. Follow me on Facebook. This is the real me. Go to www.facebook.com/cocolec.
2. Visit www.cocosyoga.com to connect and join my online community.
3. For feedback or ideas, please email to me at wakeuppotential@gmail.com.

To Live as Long as I Can as Best as I Can

Eric Guttmann

Sometimes you know the exact time and place that changed your life. In my case this happened as a Naval Flight Officer conducting an airborne combat reconnaissance mission overland Iraq on board the EP-3E Signals Intelligence (SIGINT) aircraft.

My crew and I were flying a mission in support of Operation IRAQI FREEDOM, when a loud beeping noise broke everyone's concentration. I looked to the flight station and saw a flurry of hands moving frantically, activating levers, and pulling circuit breakers.

Clearly, something had gone wrong.

The Electronic Warfare Commander (EWAC) announced the following on the aircraft's Intercommunication System (ICS), "Crew, this is the EWAC speaking, we have just lost an engine. This requires us to descend to MANPAD range (Man Portable Air Defense System). Please man all the windows and if you see a corkscrew smoke trail heading towards the aircraft let us know immediately so we can take evasive action." The corkscrew smoke trail would mean that we were being fired upon. A sudden sinking feeling came over the pit of my stomach. "So this is what it feels like when everything goes terribly wrong," I thought to myself. This happened in August 2004, a time when those captured were beheaded on YouTube. What happened next was a surreal experience.

At first I was nervous and felt all my energy drained. Upon the inevitability of death as part of life in the Naval Service and as a consequence of conducting wartime airborne reconnaissance missions, I accepted my fate "If it is my time, then it is my time."

Upon letting go, a strange calm and sense of peace came over me and my life literally flashed before my eyes. While in real time it must have been a second or a fraction of a second, in some other dimension of time I was able to relive my WHOLE life. I also experienced the effect of all my actions on others. Whether good or bad, I understood what others felt as a result of my actions and behavior, like a perfect ledger that accounted for all the second and third order effects of my actions.

My mind then projected into the future and I could see two men dressed in Service Dress Blues knocking on the door to my home and letting my wife know that I was either dead or captured. I felt her anguish, fear and pain at both losing me and having to raise a family on her own.

— "DO YOU HAVE THE THREE ENGINE MINIMUM RISK ROUTING?!?!?!"

The pilot screamed at me.

— "WHAT IS THE THREE ENGINE MINIMUM RISK ROUTING?!?!?!"

The pilot screamed at me again and brought me back to reality. We had just lost an engine, and I needed to provide a heading away from Baghdad and into the pre-determined egress route.

— "WE NEED A HEADING NOW! WHAT IS THE HEADING?"

The pilot screamed again and this time, my training kicked in and I started going through all my procedures. I got on headset and said the following:

— "Flight, Nav turn to heading 270."

I started reprogramming all of the aircraft's navigation systems and monitored our flight path. When we hit our first waypoint on the egress route the EWAC says to the other pilot and myself on the private ICS net, "Yeah, she is a stable bird. I tell you, if you have to lose an engine in any plane, no better one to take you back home alive that this one right here."

When we landed everyone chuckled about it, but I was aware that I had just experienced something that we are supposed to experience at the end of our lives. The more I reflected on it the more I realized the one distinct desire emanating from the bottom of my soul.

— I WANT TO LIVE!

This was not a thought, observation, or an emotion.

This was a SOUL DECISION.

I wanted to live and would start to take immediate action to make the best of this second chance I was given. Just like I reprogrammed the aircraft's navigation systems I would reprogram my mind, body, and spirit to LIVE.

I was at the Base Exchange when I intuitively picked an Inside Kung-Fu magazine looking for the first step in this decision. As I perused the pages of the magazine I saw an ad for a Qigong course by a guy named Peter Ragnar. I had done extensive Qigong training and Chen style Taijiquan during my college years and knew firsthand of its life enhancing effects. I immediately ordered the course and saw that Peter had a lot of books and materials on open-ended longevity.

This started a process of experimenting on myself and others as human guinea pigs to do everything possible to, "Live as Long as You Can as Best as You Can."

After incorporating Qigong back into my life, I really started to look at nutrition and how it affects health, strength, and longevity. The first component was proper hydration. After reading about the effects of chronic dehydration and what it takes to be fully hydrated I conducted a simple experiment upon myself, for 30 days I would ONLY drink one gallon of distilled water a day. That's right, no juices, colas, or alcohol. Every payday I would go to the grocery store and get 15 gallons of distilled water. At the end of the 30 days I was working out at the base gym when I ran out of my distilled water. Since the "trial period" had passed I went to the water fountain to take a sip. For the first time in my life I literally felt and tasted all the "impurities" in the water. The taste was so disgusting I literally had to spit it out. From that day forward I stopped all colas and alcohol and resolved to drink only water. Once I committed to this approach I bought a home distiller and started distilled my own water.

While much has been written about nutrition, there are multiple and often contradictory opinions on what constitutes the healthiest diet. However, one thing is clear, healthy food is to be found as close as possible to its natural state and free of man-made chemicals. I had already been a vegetarian twice in my life and it did not provide the advantages I was looking for, but drastically increasing the amount of raw fresh organic produce we consume is a sure way to increase our health and guarantee a steady stream of enzymes and minerals to process any animal meats we do decide to eat. Instead of shopping for food based on price I started shopping for food based on nutrition. I started visiting the farmer's markets and getting to know the people that grow my food. Is it more expensive? Yes. Is your health worth it? Absolutely.

This led me to one my experiments in nutrition which is to eat for your hormones. As was explained to me by my good friend Stephen Santangelo, "You can control the rate of fat storage for the day by what you eat for breakfast." I asked him what this meant and he explained the role of insulin in the body and how when we trigger insulin we also trigger other hormones that are responsible for fat storage and hunger. He mentioned that if we can wait until lunch to turn on insulin then we are consistently preventing turning on the fat mechanism in the morning and that over time this will result in fat loss. I decided to try a little experiment where I would wait until dinner to turn on insulin via diet and lost 10 pounds without exercising any willpower or changing my exercise routine. However, since I did not want to keep on losing weight I started turning insulin back at lunchtime and have regained 10 pounds of muscle. Because I was using the same training method during both periods where I lost and then re-gained the weight it became clear to me that the number one factor for fat loss is diet. Hence the popular term, "You can't out train a bad diet," which means that you can't make up for a crappy diet doing extra exercise.

The biggest benefit of eating for your hormones is how easy it becomes to stick to healthy eating habits as opposed to requiring huge amounts of willpower to "eat clean" and then beating yourself up when "cheat." This has helped a lot of my clients, from fifty year old women re-starting their careers to experienced martial artists with world-wide commitments. This approach works because you do not have to give up your favorite foods or adopt a particular eating regimen like vegan or paleo, rather you incorporate PRINCIPLES into your eating regimen.

Fixing your nutrition will do wonders for your health, strength, and longevity because it starts to build self-reliance and fights the "false belief" that decrepitude is inevitable. As people start to take full ownership of their food intake this allows them to take action to take full ownership of their bodies.

Taking full ownership of your body means regaining the mobility and voluntary control of all the joints in your body. Depending on your current state of health, this may take a couple of days or a couple of months. However, once you regain full mobility, a lot of everyday aches and pains go away, you are able to keep better posture, you recover faster from workouts and training injuries, and you are able to learn physical skills faster. Also, full mobility is what allows a person to train safely. Why? Because when you do not have full mobility in a joint, then the joint on top or below that compromised joint has to bear extra weight and deal with unnatural shearing forces.

Just as compromised joints apply shearing forces on the body, so does extra weight. One of the most recurring requests I get from clients is help with fat loss, especially fat loss after forty. They confide in me their frustration because they try the approach they used successfully in their twenties and thirties, which was to curtail calories and increase exercise, but to their dismay it no longer seems to work now that they are in their forties and the weight never comes off.

One of the keys which has helped the people I work with the most is the correct use of liver cleanses for health, longevity, and fat loss. While the fact that over-consumption of calories will lead to fat accumulation is understood by most, what is not known is that the body encapsulates whatever it deems harmful or toxic in fat to protect the body from coming in contact with it. The body does this with the notion that at some point in time the liver will be able to safely break down this harmful material.

Unfortunately, that day never comes.

Today's "modern" society blasts the human body with fake and processed foods, more sugar than at any other time in human history, hundreds of thousands of man-made chemicals the body cannot process, stress, pollution, and over-medication of prescription drugs, just to name a few. This causes the liver to be constantly overburdened. The body keeps encapsulating these substances in fat as a survival mechanism. If there is alcohol and/or recreational drug use then the liver is further set back.

For people over 40, this is the bottleneck when it comes to weight and fat loss. A proper liver cleanse will start clearing all this debris from decades of neglect and abuse and will get you on the path to radiant health and achieving a healthy weight. I have had people drop up to 200 "stones" in one liver cleanse. The benefits go beyond weight loss as I had one lady with psoriasis tell me that 75% of it cleared overnight with just one liver cleanse. The liver cleanse I practice and teach only requires organic olive oil, an organic grape fruit, and Epsom salts.

Once you regain the full use of your body, get your nutrition in order, and start getting your liver back into shape then we can move on to exciting things like using exercise to boost Testosterone and Human Growth Hormone production.

This was the result of me asking, "what if every exercise session at the gym could be converted into both a therapy and rejuvenation session?"

Instead of "killing it" at the gym you would be training for health and longevity by focusing on hormones. Specifically - how to boost Testosterone and Human Growth Hormone through exercise. While these are tailored approaches based on each individual person, the short answer is that you have to train in such a way to create an adaptation response that results in either the production of Testosterone or Human Growth Hormone. If you can check your ego at the door and focus on these principles then you realize that you do not have to spend 2 hours a day in the gym 6 days a week. In fact, if you are over 40 this will work AGAINST you. Now in my 40's I am much more athletic than in my 20's, it may take me longer to recover from hard workouts, but I can see myself maintaining my vitality and zest for life indefinitely as long as I keep on following and honoring these principles.

My father was a Greco-Roman wrestler in Hungary when he was a young man. When I was seven years old I noticed that he did exercises every morning. I asked him why he did it and he told me that his Eastern European wrestling coach shared the wisdom of, "if you do something every day, then every day you will be able to do it."

Every day I reset my body to full mobility and am pain free, and I can teach you how you can do this too. If you do this, which can take as little as six minutes a day, then every day for the rest of your life you will have full mobility. I train twice a week and intend to do so for the rest of my life to keep healthy levels of Testosterone and Human Growth Hormone, and I can teach you so you can too. Every day I strategically spend time in the morning sun to increase my vitamin D levels to reduce the probability of cancer, fully hydrate my body, and avoid turning insulin on at breakfast, and I can teach you so you can too.

There are a myriad of more things that I do and teach, but now the ball is in your court. If you want to learn simple strategies that have been reality tested on myself and others then reach out to me and let's work out a plan, because anything I have done, you can too!

About the Author

Eric Guttmann

Health-Strength-Longevity Consultant & Best-Selling Author

I help people to "Live as Long as You Can as Best as You Can" and have worked with athletes, martial artist, busy professionals, housewives, and people who have lost their health and vitality and want to gain it back to LIVE long, happy, and healthy lives. One of the most successful programs I run is the "Fat Loss After 40 for Men Only" and "Fat Loss After 40 for Women Only" online coaching group.

After conducting all sorts of experiments on myself and others as human Guinea pigs, I started developing a definite set of reality tested principles and practices that enhance your health, strength, quality of life, mindset, vitality, longevity and freedom.

More importantly, I realized that HABITS trump WILLPOWER and the most important factor for success is CONSISTENCY. By working with the mind and body instead of trying to impose your will on it, you do the right things consistently—allowing you to save precious time and energy for the achievement of your goals and dreams. I want to offer you the opportunity to learn everything that is required to take full ownership of your life.

To be able to implement your will and the desires of your spirit you need to have a physical and mental vehicle that is strong and resilient enough to make those desires a reality.

Get in touch today to sign up for the Fat Loss After 40 program.
Want to start now? Get my mobility course at:
www.ericguttmann.com/moving-freely/

Active Duty Naval Officer, Published Author, & Health and Longevity Coach

www.EricGuttmann.com

Facebook: ericguttmann

Rebel With a Big Heart: Connect to Your True Self and Create a Life You Love

Kimberly Crigger

It was the summer of 1975 and my family had just moved to a small town in Northwest Ohio. My sisters and I spent most of our days exploring the backyard and the woods looking for treasures. Playing in nature was a magical experience. I loved being surrounded by trees, listening to birds, breathing in fresh air and taking in the smell of the earth. We went outside, rain or shine, created games, and moved our bodies. It was an innocent, slower-paced time in life, and these memories remain dear to my heart. I loved feeling so free and treasured the connection I felt with my sisters and baby brother. When I spent time in the woods, I felt grounded and connected to my inner being; my soul self.

Fast forward to my college years; while I experienced some great moments, what I remember most is feeling lost and completely stressed out. The pressure of countless reading assignments, projects, papers, and final exams sent me into overwhelm. I felt powerless, which sometimes led to bad habits and poor decisions. After graduation, the next step was to apply for jobs that would lead to a "career." Once again, overwhelm kicked in because I didn't know what I wanted. At the time, my vision was clouded but I see now that I was going through the motions without a clear plan, hoping for the best. Feelings of discouragement lasted for a few years until I settled into a job as an insurance underwriter. I didn't love it, but appreciated the stability and consistent income.

Ten years later, I married and started a family. Life was good and we were blessed with two healthy children. I was a full-time mom and I felt like I had a purpose. Unfortunately, my tendency to feel anxious kicked in during my kids' toddler years. It didn't help that my marriage was showing signs of trouble either. I tried everything I could think of to manage my stress: shopping, drinking wine, practicing yoga, and even running marathons. While I thought these "coping strategies" were working, they did not help my marriage. In 2009, I finalized the divorce; it one of the most devastating moments in my life.

Here I was again feeling overwhelm and anxious about my future. I knew that this was a pivotal life lesson, not to be treated lightly. In fact, I learned that major life changes such as divorce can lead to chronic stress, which is linked to causing physical and emotional illness. According to the medical site, www.Helpguide. org, "Chronic stress disrupts nearly every system in your body. It can suppress your immune system, upset your digestive and reproductive systems, increase your risk of heart attack and stroke and speed up the aging process. It can even rewire the brain, leaving you more vulnerable to anxiety, depression, and other mental health issues." According to the American Institute of Stress, 77% of Americans alone experience physical symptoms caused by stress and 73% experience psychological symptoms. Living with chronic stress reduces our chance of living a healthy, vibrant life that we all deserve. Unfortunately, most people are not aware that they have the power to change their situation and continue to live in fear, doubt and general unhappiness.

Luckily, months before my divorce was final I completed my

second yoga teacher training and developed a daily meditation practice. This. Saved. My. Sanity. Every time I meditated or practiced yoga I felt a sense of calm wash over me. I noticed that I was less reactive to emotional triggers and became more aware of my critical thoughts and self-judgment. I was healing physically, emotionally and spiritually and bringing more confidence and clarity into my life. My transformation inspired me so much that I wanted to share my new passion with everyone, so, I taught several yoga classes a week and still had the freedom to be with my kids. In my spare time, I studied other spiritual modalities like Reiki, shamanic healing, astrology, and the Law of Attraction, to name a few. I could not take in enough information through books, videos, classes and workshops. I finally found my calling!

Teaching these concepts intuitively felt like the perfect choice since it expanded my life and I realized I could help others do the same. Both of my parents were teachers and I believe I was destined to teach, but my newly found passion was definitely not the norm. I have always been a cross between a conformist and a rebel. Others around me did not always understand my love for yoga, breath-work and meditation with its esoteric, mystical qualities, but I knew there were practical and grounding features as well and this combination made me feel connected to myself again.

As the months passed, I continued to merge with my true self. I was reminded of my harmonious childhood days playing and daydreaming in the woods with my sisters. I saw through my illusions and the world around me opened up. I realized that I had finally found my soul purpose in teaching others to help themselves and awaken to their inner wisdom so that they too could feel the joy and freedom in their life.

One of the most important concepts I have learned in the last decade is that our thoughts and beliefs create our experience. If we focus clearly on what is wanted rather than unwanted, we will create the life we desire. We are **powerful** creators. If you don't believe me, think of a time when you were so excited and laser focused on something that you wanted, whether it was a new pair of jeans or a job promotion, and it came into your reality. Did you feel excited knowing it was on the way? How did it feel once you received it? You most likely felt connected to your heart, took inspired action, and had a sense of anticipation in knowing it would happen. On the other hand, look at the situations in your life that you aren't so thrilled about. Do you think it's possible that your thoughts, feelings, and beliefs about this topic have something to do with where you are now?

You have the power to choose! You are an amazing, intelligent, infinite being and you have the ability to create happiness, freedom, and vitality over sadness, fear, and mediocrity. My goal is to guide you from going down the road of disappointment, so I've created an easy five-step method to help you design the life you love. I call it the **Living (A.W.A.K.E.) Method.**

(A)wareness is the key.

This is the first step towards your emotional, mental, and spiritual growth. In fact, it applies to the physical world as well. If you're not aware of how your body feels in yoga, for instance, you're just going through the motions and missing part of the experience. By becoming more aware, you will begin to observe your own reactions to certain situations, people, and places. Eventually you will notice repetitive thoughts, words, and gestures. You'll also become more sensitive to smells, sounds, and physical sensations. Awareness is a key component to awakening and lifting you out of the coma-like state that comes from living in a fast-paced, competitive, and desensitized world.

The frightening part for most is uncovering those deep-rooted beliefs that have been buried beneath our well-mannered façade for years. No worries! Facing our shadow emotions can be unnerving and this step to the awakening process is often the biggest deterrent for most people on their healing journey. It's understandable since many of us have been raised or influenced by others who judged our mistakes and flaws and were therefore punished, blamed, or embarrassed. If you did not experience any of this, then consider yourself an enlightened being! However, I'm going to bet that most of you have gone through feelings of fear, anxiety, rejection, or loneliness at one time or another in your life.

With heightened awareness you may notice judgmental thoughts like, "I could have done better," "I'm disgusted with my body," or "I'm not enough." From this space, notice how you feel and perhaps ask yourself, "Is this how I want to feel?" When you experience emotional discomfort, it's the key indicator that you're out of alignment with your inner being, your true, and all-knowing self. It's super simple; just slow down and notice your repetitive thoughts, feelings, and beliefs.

Some easy and effective ways to tap into your own **awareness** are:

1. Practice daily meditation. Keep it simple and commit to 10 to 15 minutes a day. This is a game changer! Daily meditation will help you reduce stress and overwhelm. You will have more clarity and confidence to make wiser choices, especially under challenging circumstances. According to The American journal of Psychiatry, a consistent meditation practice literally reduces the density of brain tissue associated with anxiety and worrying.

2. Go into nature and spend time connecting to Mother Earth. Walk your dog, go hiking, tend to your garden, whatever it is that motivates you, and explore the outdoors. "Looking at beauty in the world is the first step of purifying the mind." Amit Ray

3. Exercise and move your body every day. It raises your endorphins, the "feel good" hormones, bringing vitality and a sense of accomplishment. Just choose something you enjoy and get moving, at least 30 minutes a day.

With more **awareness** of your thoughts, actions and environment, you'll gain a deeper understanding of who you really are, how to navigate through the muck, and step into a brighter version of your life. What you focus on repeatedly is drawn to you, so why not be aware of your thoughts and learn to focus on what you want to bring into your life? This brings us to the next step.

(W)hat do you want?

What do you want to bring into your life right now? What have you been longing for hasn't happened yet? Do you know what you want to experience in your life? It's like the old saying, "You can't get there if you don't know where you're going." This is so true. It's exactly what I was doing in my earlier years! I simply had forgotten that I was in charge of my own destiny and allowed my anxiety to take the lead. By slowing down, connecting to your feelings and desires, you're able to dive deeper into discovering your true passions and begin the process of designing your dream life.

Yes, you can create anything and have been creating wanted and unwanted scenarios in your life since you were born. When you know exactly what you want, whether it's a new car or a soul mate relationship, simply focus your thoughts on the details of what it looks and feels like to have in your life. You can start by connecting with your heart and asking three questions in each area of your life:

1. What Do I want?
2. Why Do I want it?
3. How do I want to feel when it's here?

By asking these questions, you will connect with your feelings and keep yourself on track towards your destination.

(A)lign with your Inner Being

This can happen simultaneously with the second step, because you determine what you'd like to manifest much faster by connecting to your wise self, also known as your inner being, your true self. This is the big YOU, the part of you that isn't always visible. When you quiet your mind and **align**, you have more clarity and feel empowered. This is the real you that taps into divine intelligence and guides from your heart. Your inner being/true self understands healthy boundaries and what path leads to the highest good for all. This isn't about pleasing others and doing what they tell you to do; rather, this is about listening to your own sacred wisdom and following the guidance. Follow your inner rebel! Once you align and connect, you are on the way to designing a life you love while creating miracles along the way.

(K)now it's on the way

Once you've set your goals and intentions and aligned with your True Self, it's time to step into trusting the Universe and **know** that your wishes are on the way. This principle is not from some fairy tale with flying Unicorns and rainbows, this is a proven Law of the Universe, called the Law of Allowing. It just means, get out of your own way, stay focused on the prize, know it's already made manifest and let go. Yes, let go, no need to obsess or practice focused visualizations for 8 hours a day! In fact, once you have determined what it is you'd like to bring to fruition and have focused with clear intention, based on how you want to feel, say, "thank you, because I know it's on the way." Step into your new reality and **know** that you are an amazing creator! When you focus on your desires and feel your way towards your vision, expect it to happen.

(E)xpand and excel.

Now that you have embodied your new reality and allowed your goals to manifest, it's time to step up and reach for more **expansion** within yourself. Spiritual growth is a never-ending endeavor, but one of the ways to catapult yourself into brilliance is to teach others what you've learned. You don't have to be a yoga teacher, life coach, or an enlightened master to be an awakened leader. Be the best version of YOU and people will notice. Lead by example. You will make a positive impact in the world when you live in the space of your highest potential.

Looking back, I am so grateful that I embraced my inner rebel and took the unconventional path to healing. The world needs more truth seekers, especially now. It is vital for the harmony of our planet that we teach future generations about the power to choose our thoughts and live with consciousness, pure potentiality and freedom. Some of the best true leaders and change makers lead with their hearts and have a mission of creating outcomes for the highest good of all. By being the best version of you and owning your expansive brilliance, you will live an amazing, fulfilling life, positively impact those around you and teach them how to live the life they love!

About the Author

Kimberly Grigger

Kim Crigger is a Quantum Success certified Law of Attraction Coach, yoga teacher, author, and conscious thought leader who has dedicated the last decade to learning the sacred teachings of yoga, meditation, and mind-body healing. Her mission is to teach others how to step in into their power and live with full consciousness, freedom, joy, and purpose.

Kim@awakenyourinnerlight.com
AwakenYourInnerLight.com

Modern Self-Liberation: Reclaiming Wellness, Purpose, and Personal Power

Frederick Entenmann

Overall, there's a murky cloud of disillusionment in reference to having a vibrant mind, body, and life. Vibrancy doesn't primarily incorporate a single element but embodies an all-encompassing commitment that integrates specific behaviors, skills, and tools. It's a holistic lifestyle that synergizes and enlivens all aspects of consciousness (MIND), health and wellness (BODY), and environment (LIFE). Unfortunately, manipulative snake-oil marketers and other self-proclaimed, hypnotic 'gurus' have engineered a false perception of wellness through 'buzzed' vibrancy, such as embracing the feeling of getting high on adrenaline, spiking your nervous system into fight or flight and telling you how "great" you are. The truth is that vibrancy isn't found through instant gratification, 'thinking' about it or popping a pill. Such deceptive information involves fraudulent mechanisms that quack-hazzardly result in depression, aging, addiction, stress, burnout, obesity, fatigue, illness, and disease for starters.

Authentic power stems from taking personal accountability. Only when we master our inner game do we become a vibrant force that flows through us, emanating outwards. Albert Einstein and Nikola Tesla have established that "everything is energy," which is transformable. For instance, have you have noticed, the quieter you are, the more connected, clear, and present you become? Unfortunately, schools neglect teaching this simple truth and also how to protect vital life force energy. Instead of being taught that one's natural state is loving kindness through open-hearted vulnerability, it's reinforced to neurotically protect oneself by creating an environment that forms walls around the intelligent heart. This mind-set only reinforces negative habits such as gossiping, finger pointing, victimization, complaining, drama and staying trapped in stories to keep one in a perpetual and chronic state of enervation, fear, and depletion.

Energy is everything! You are only given so much in this lifetime and you can't refill it at the pump. This is why establishing boundaries of guarding your reserves are so critical. Just remember this: Reactiveness equals power leakage. Every time you over-react, this causes an actual biological attachment that drives those emotions into your physiology.

So whether it's losing oneself in sports, a career, or relationships, conserving and guarding your energy force is an essential tool that requires legitimate life skills and proper awareness. Sweeping emotions under the rug, avoiding confrontation, or engaging in passive aggressiveness are all learned behaviors that decimate your energy and cause systemic blockages. For example, if you have an egotistical jerk for a coach, don't allow the attachment to words or unforeseen outcomes drain you. The same applies to a friend, a teacher, spouse, or a boss. If things become too negative, detach and leave; it is that simple.

Taking personal responsibility for oneself leads to the inherent ability to adapt and overcome any given situation because it squashes conventional attachments and makes one less easily deceived or taken advantage of. This also prevents your self-power from ever getting to the point to where it can become corrupt. You see, when you align your heart first instead of your ego, your priorities shift from the mental to a sacred connection with your immediate environment. Physiology is important, but transitioning long-established doctrinal principles into holistic wellness methods that address comprehensive emotional, psychological, inner strength, wisdom and your body's intelligent capacity creates that immense high-vibe that everyone inherently desires.

What the mind expects, it finds; it's a self-fulfilling prophecy. For instance, when you are self-assured that accomplishment is within your grasp, you relax and look for solutions rather than dwell on problems; its a sweet spot where you want to be. In essence, flow is when you naturally manifest positive situations or outcomes and disregard thoughts related to uncertainty, failure, or roadblocks. Truly, if you anticipate joy, health, happiness, and accomplishment, then you will most likely experience each one. Freedom constitutes living without fear (thought) or emotional baggage (soul). Leonardo da Vinci said, "For once you have tasted flight, you will walk the earth with your eyes turned skywards, for there you have been and there you will long to return." Self-love is a practice that cultivates one's true self and when alignment occurs, you too will spread your wings. At heart, you will find that you just need to get out of your own way and become enlivened by big-picture thinking. Moreover, cultivate a sustainable sacred space inside yourself that consistently feeds your imagination, where dreams are allowed to soar.

Authentic happiness is not a secret formula but stems from being in sync with heart alignment. Yet we are taught that our brain is the know-all, do-all; that thinking or increasing your IQ is the pinnacle of genius. Did you know that just by being quiet your heartbeat could match the electromagnetic current of the planet? That's right, according to recent research, the electrical field as measured in an electrocardiogram is about sixty times greater than the amplitude brain waves recorded on an electroencephalogram (EEG). This should be of interest because truth and wisdom entails tapping into your bioelectrical heart intelligence. Currently, growing evidence suggests energetic interactions involving the heart may underlie intuition and important aspects of human consciousness, not by over-achieving on some standardized test that falsely labels one as intelligent.

No wall is big enough to withstand the power of your heart. "Follow your bliss and the universe will open doors where there were only walls." Plato said that we do not actually learn anything that we are born to create. Instead, the more we feel, the more we can create. Creating makes us feel vibrant and alive. It's familiar to your soul! This single process helps you let go of societal expectations and embrace your destiny. From this sacred space, you are free to discover your bliss; your life's passion.

Socrates states that "We already know." It's the modern learning model that unravels your innate wisdom and knowledge. You see, when you discover what truly inspires, you can then make that the basis for your personal hero's journey. Purpose is what gets one excited to live, contribute, and create. Believe me, it's certainly not your fault if you are bored or frustrated with your relationships, career or schooling. No amount of wealth or career success will ever fulfill you if it is not in alignment with your purpose, and ZERO amount of regurgitation of test answers, certifications, or degrees will ever bring complete gratification to the human soul.

Growth transcends beyond the self-limitations of routine. Sure, the first days, weeks, or months are difficult with change. Unfortunately, many view change as negative because it challenges regular routines and systematically ingrained, dogmatic beliefs. However, in retrospect, it is extremely unsettling when you finally get out of incapacitating habits that have gotten you to where you are at in the first place. I often ask, "So when do you plan to take a stand and overcome your self-limiting patterns and beliefs that cripple your dreams and visions?" It takes more energy to keep the walls of resistance up than just to allow them down. Just get out of your own way!

Being present, grounded, and experiencing the full-dimensional verve for life is the intuitively desirable way to live. Everybody wants answers yet it's not about information, per se. Divine magic occurs through eliminating distractions, creating, and than executing upon taking action. Think back to when you were a child; remember just doing? Just let go of chasing the answers as if it will bring you complete fulfillment. Yes, the answers are already inside you. It's the hypnotic confusion associated with comparing, competing, or commiserating that often takes you away from the present, leaving you overwhelmed with undesirable feelings. Do you remember flowing with ideas, dreams, and visions at the age of five? It takes practice to unplug and get back to that state of mind. Only when you learn to love yourself fully can you truly let go, slow time, and embrace the present as it was meant to be. It is only then that you can feel energized and fully alive.

It is common knowledge that your body requires daily movement to remain healthy, invigorated, and functional. However, the types of movement and overall physical exertion required remains to be subject to debate. Presently, there is an emergence of studies revealing how many ailments respond well to natural therapies such as yoga and breath work. Breath work aids in losing unwanted weight, getting sleep, improving digestion, lowering blood pressure, enhancing the immune system, improving mood, increasing mental clarity, eliminating addictions like smoking or drinking, looking and feeling more youthful and vibrant, increasing lifespan, and giving people more energy. You see, your breath alone kindles life force and can release any trapped, repressed, or blocked energy force that obstructs your energy field.

Research also continues to discover more about the adverse effects of stress on our bodies and minds. Within the last few decades, yoga, an ancient preventative Eastern practice, is now considered an alternative therapy for a multitude of ailments in the Western world. Yoga not only combats stress, but it also provides extra health benefits that allow the body to heal itself naturally, such as increasing brain neurotransmitters (responsible for mood and pain response), reduces blood pressure, heart rate, and inflammation (a leading cause of heart and vascular diseases). For starters, the results are profound and encouraging for depression, anxiety, addiction, stress, inflammation, and arthritis.

Part of the modernization of yoga was the view of the practice as just another form of exercise or relaxation technique. Personally, I find yoga beneficial and unique in that it combines the advantages of meditation and exercise. Holding true to its root word yuj, meaning, "to unite," bringing the mind and body into harmony. Once you realize yoga is using the body as a means to create space where you were once stuck and unravel the layers of protection you've constructed around your heart, you also increase self-love.

You cannot get any more from life than what you bring to it. Thus, you cannot get any more benefit from any fitness, exercise, breath work, or yoga than what you bring to it. If you exclusively bring the physical benefits of the body as a central focus in your practice, then that is the most you can get from it. However, when you incorporate the body and mind, then you extend your life benefits into a whole new element. Fusing the mind, body, heart, and soul synergizes your practice, shifting into the Fourth dimension, where yoga fulfills its original purpose.

So how does America lead the world in depression? For starters, in addition to the lack of quality food, clean air, pure water, proper sleep, and daily movement, most have become desensitized and hollowed-out into an all-consuming cavity programmed for a false sense of fulfillment via consumerizing instant gratification. On a larger scale, embracing artificial relaxation or escape vehicles via prescription psychoactive medications, tranquilizers, chemically laden, processed franken-foods, alcohol, drugs, television programming, computers, video games, career-work, or sports obsessions, life suddenly becomes a coping mechanism for ignoring pain, rather than removing the root of it.

No matter how long you ignore the enemy, the enemy moves closer every moment, solving zero problems and gaining more power. You see, that which is used as a way to kill the pain also becomes the source of more pain. That which is adopted to avoid pain perpetually sustains, prolongs, and reinforces the pain. All the devices adopted either to suppress pain or to avoid pain are like throwing explosives onto a fire; it only makes the field of unconsciousness extend, creating greater insensitivity.

We all have the natural power to heal our bodies. I challenge you to disconnect from technological distractions as often as possible and reconnect with your immediate surroundings. The notion that trees affect us on an energetic basis is not new. For example, we know instinctively after walking in a forest or swimming in the ocean that we are calmer and more relaxed than when we entered. Nature provides this bridge to wellness by offering a suitable healing environment. You don't need to read research articles to know this. Just take action and get out into it! I promise it's an absolute game-changer.

Everyone always inquires about reaching new levels of life vibrancy and my answer is, "Just be quiet!" Intentional silence puts us in a state of reflection and disengages our intellectual mind. Quietness, or the practice of ~quietude~, is the elixir for mental blocks. Lao Tzu says, "Stillness reveals the secrets of eternity." During silence, the mind is best able to cultivate a form of mindful intention that later motivates us to take action. At this point, ask yourself questions such as, "If anything were possible, what would I welcome or create in my life?" or, "When I'm feeling most courageous and inspired, what do I want to offer the world?" or, "When I'm honest about how I suffer, what do I want to make peace with?" Removing critical mind chatter allows positive emotions and our imagination to build a subconscious intention and adds focus and purpose to our goals.

It goes without saying that the brain is an extremely complex organ, but like muscles, it benefits from rest (I'm not talking about sleeping in until noon). The creative process includes a crucial stage called incubation, where all the ideas we've been exposed to get to meet, mingle, marinate, and subsequently produce an "Aha" moment. You have to literally disengage from the work at hand and take a rest in order for an idea to essentially incubate.

Again, only when we slow ourselves waaaaaaaay down can we truly connect to our hearts. Too much thinking is detrimental to output and blocks flow; slowing down creates connectedness and presence. Setting aside regular times throughout your day to disengage, sit in silence, and just mentally rest is monumental for clarity and focus. This eases your cerebral cortex and boosts your ability to process information. Carving out as little as 15 minutes to even sit in your car and visualize peaceful scenery (rainforest, snow-falling, beach, etc.) is a good start. Additionally, this thickens grey matter in your brain and can be done anywhere!

Our present day lifestyles have benefited us in numerous ways but incur unfortunate consequences. The deteriorating nutritional value of the American diet, lack of physical activity, and chronic high-stress levels assassinate overall health and wellness. Heart disease, hypertension, diabetes, cancers and prescription drugs continue to rise epidemically; even among children, adolescents, and young adults. Remember, one of your greatest assets is taking personal accountability over your life. Nobody feeds you but YOU. Processed or synthetically enhanced franken-food sources hold little to zero nutritional benefit and do not serve their original intent. So why support it?

A diet grounded on fresh, living food radically improves your health and immediate environment. There is no one size fits all diet per se, as everyone is different. However, consuming raw food is the number one action that nourishes and maximizes health through preserving enzymes. Animals that live in the wild don't suffer from chronic degenerative diseases, as do humans and domesticated animals. It is a striking fact that all other species, without exception, eat their foods raw, whereas the overwhelming majority of people do not. It's a striking truth that when animals are fed cooked foods, they too begin to suffer chronic degenerative diseases.

Fasting is a powerful way to conserve and redirect enzyme potential as ultimately you stop producing digestive enzymes. This energy diverts the metabolic sphere of operations, which includes an increased rate of autolysis as well as a breakdown and elimination of fatty deposits, incomplete proteins, and other toxic material in the system. Thus, the enzymes become a rejuvenating power for you because your natural body bacteria have an opportunity to add plenty of their enzymes to your system, increasing your total enzymatic force. Working with a juicing expert, I experienced the first-hand medicinal effects that raw juices have on an eclectic group of individuals ranging from executives, professional athletes, yogis, and foodies all looking for that high-vibration holistic edge. When we fast on water or juices, we provide a substantial rest to our digestive enzyme systems, taking the burden off of our collective enzyme pool. In effect, this takes our mind, body, and life frequency to an extremely high level.

When your actions, habits, and desires are in alignment

with your purpose, you too can experience complete mind, body and life harmony. You are a resilient phenomenon! With energy as a key enabler, your thoughts and actions in the here and now are acute determinants of reality and destiny. Above all, vibrancy prevails when you replace processed franken-junk with proper nourishment of untampered food, clean water, fresh air, empowered thoughts, daily exercise and soul stimulation. Sure, routine provides great comfort, but comfort naturally manifests stagnancy. So, if you're frustrated with the direction of your life, just try something different and confront your fears. Stop running, head right into the storm and boldly embody what you want! Because all in all, every single moment is a gift; a monumental opportunity to enhance your life's journey that is readily available by liberating yourself from fear, transcending away from uncreative habits and evolving forward with monumental expansiveness.

About the Author

Frederick Entenmann

A former professional athlete, bestselling author *Surviving Sports And The Game Of Life*, consultant, and host of the MIND BODY LIFE show on Global Voice Radio, Frederick Entenmann helps Professional Athletes WIN the game of life.

Facebook: Frederick Entenmann & Team MIND BODY LIFE
Instagram: frederickentenmann
LinkedIn: Frederick Entenmann
Twitter: FEntenmann

Discovering the Fountain of Youth

Jimmy Gleason

In December of 2015 I had gone home to Michigan for Christmas in need of love and emotional healing. Earlier that year in March, I had suffered the traumatic loss of my best friend. I was beginning to eat healthier already trying to eat as many alkaline foods as I could. I had discovered that milk was not very good for me and wasn't natural to our bodies. I switched to organic almond milk and noticed that I was feeling better. For about a year I had switched my diet to eating primarily organic meats, eggs, and vegetables, along with healthy cereals. While in Michigan, I went shopping and made sure I bought all the healthy food I was used to eating in California.

During this time, I also didn't gorge myself on all the sweets like I had always done, but instead ate much smaller samples. I began to notice that I didn't get tired like I always did after eating, while everyone else became very sleepy. This is when my eyes first really began to open up to how lots of sweets and fatty meals wear your body down. I was waking up to the harmful effects of high amounts of sugar. Toward the last week of my vacation, I began to be aware in my spirit that I needed to go on a cleanse from eating meat and high amounts of sugar. I had heard about how red meat especially could sit in your large intestine and rot inside you, not being digested for months. That was my impetus for getting unclean food like that out of my intestinal system.

Four or five days before I was to fly back to Southern California, I received a call from my new friend, Steven. He had been doing a lot of business travel and needed a place to rent for about a month or so before he went on more travels. I had moved back to the house where my friend had died. After three months of being away from that house, I welcomed the possibility of having a friend stay with me so I wasn't alone there. I flew back a day before New Year's and as soon as I walked in the house, I smelled food. As I walked into the kitchen I never saw healthier food and vegetables in my life. There was Steven with a giant smile on his face, cutting everything up like a world class chef.

As I began to talk with Steven about the display of food that was in front of me I spontaneously blurted out, "I can't believe I came in the house and all this food was waiting for me! I was just a week ago beginning to talk about how I needed to go on a cleanse and here you are with cleansing food already prepared for me and you had no idea I was planning to do this." I realized in my heart I was attracting this. It was obvious to me. My journey to the highest levels of health and vitality began that first day of January 2016. What a great way to start the year!

It was a big change for me to be eating vegetables, fruit, and no meat. I really began to enjoy the camaraderie of eating healthy and discovering new secrets along the way. Steven had already been in this health mode for about four months and shared with me how he felt way more energy and mental clarity. It made me want to see how eating this way would affect me. After about a week I noticed a lot more energy. In addition, I was also doing jumping exercises with my hands above my head, which I learned cleaned out my lymph nodes. They retain excess bile which, if not discarded from the body, can eventually make you sick. To aide me in getting better results, I jumped on a small trampoline.

The second week back, we had a guy from Brazil stay with us named Randall. He came into our energy circle of health and healing and we all went on this powerful journey together. Every day we would take turns making the meals and sharing our philosophies about fitness, friends and positive thinking. It was powerful to see Randall transform and open up about his life and things he had been through. Changing our eating habits also opened our minds to making better choices about having like-minded friends and also moving toward discovering what our true purpose in life was. We wanted to explore what we were truly passionate about and made to do on this earth.

As the days and months went by, I learned more important nuggets of how to obtain optimal health. One important change I made was to stop eating cereal in the morning. Most cereal has lots of sugar in it and ones that I thought were healthy had way too much sugar. When I stopped eating the cereal, I noticed my energy levels went way up. I learned I was addicted to the sugar in cereal and that's why all my life I ate it almost every day. I was in the matrix of unhealthy food with my cravings for cereal. I was literally addicted. This was one of the first unhealthy foods I started getting rid of along with homogenized milk to get me out of the vicious cycle of unhealthy dead matrix food. Steven and I began to talk about how cereal and milk or two of the food items that were promoted as healthy all our lives but actually were not good for us. I begin to realize we were all being taught a lie.

The next phase I began to delve into was getting rid of inflammation. I had tightness and inflammation all throughout my body. My Achilles tendon was so tight, as was my lower and upper back; I thought it was just me getting older. Along with eating organic food, my new theory was that all these high sugar foods and meats that had hormones pumped into them were causing this unhealthy anomaly in my body. To get rid of the inflammation I had found in my research that raw garlic cloves could get rid of my body's inflammation. I started to eat one garlic clove as my only food source in the morning so it could have its full effect. Sure enough, my body started to go through various stages of eradicating my body of inflammation.

It seemed like this nasty residue from the sugars and hormones had been stored in my body and joints and now I could feel it all being pushed out of my body. I couldn't help but think of how garlic was known to repel vampires but now I realized for me it was getting these harmful substances out of my body. I realized that vampires were not to be feared but these hormone-saturated foods and sugar-filled treats were the real enemy. I was most pleased when I noticed my Achilles tendon on my left foot loosen up. In fact, one day while walking to teach my Sunday morning tennis class, I felt a big pop go off in my left Achilles. At first, I thought that I had torn that tendon. For a brief moment, I feared the worst. As I slowly moved around, I realized it didn't hurt but that my Achilles tendon had loosened even more. One of the parents said as I was walking around that it was inflammation leaving my body. In my heart I knew they were right and began to get very excited about my new discovery. I was being given a new lease on life.

As I went deeper into these new realms of health, I felt an awakening in my spirit and in my whole being. The Fountain of Youth was there for the taking! My imagination, spontaneity, joy, and energy levels began to renew. Depression began to fade away increasingly like a distant memory. Instead of reacting to life's quandaries, I began to commune in what I saw was a higher state of consciousness where dreams were voiced regularly and then acted upon until they became reality. So much laughter and creativity was in the air every day. We were being kids again. The beauty of this new dimension we both found was that it was always there for us; we just had to open our hearts to it. There was a new truth that we had found and it carried us to a place of vitality, freedom, and joy we had never experienced.

I began to search for new levels of health. I had heard of the power of juicing and purchased my first juicer. I was at Whole Foods one day and took a picture of their juicing combinations. Combinations like Green Giant and the detox began to revitalize my energy levels even further and my brain functioned at a much higher capacity. It's as if I was doing a science experiment on myself and became totally fascinated with the beauty of my own metamorphosis. Again, the Fountain of Youth emerged. It was real. It felt like my cells were dancing!

As I began to discover this new life force of nutrition that seemed to hidden from me all my life, I began to realize I was attracting healers and healing information. I began to realize God's divine hand moved these precious pieces of knowledge into place for a purpose that was larger than me. A new piece of God's health matrix that I was introduced to was the power of deep diaphragm in breathing. In my research I found that this was one of the best ways to get unhealthy toxins out of the body and also a great way to oxygenate the whole body.

I actually learned this from one of our coauthors, Wim Hof, whose YouTube videos I had been looking at. I started doing 20 to 30 deep diaphragmatic breaths and then I would hold my breath for up to a minute, then take one deep breath in and hold for 30 seconds. (I almost passed out the first time I did this.) The very first time I did the breathing exercises, I began to feel changes in my body I had never felt before. In my lower back it began to loosen up right away. I felt more energy throughout my body and I also could feel the toxins being removed from my body, especially the chest area.

Every day since I first started deep breathing, I became more conscious of how important it was to take time out every morning to love on myself and project my destiny through an affirmation. My morning always begins with spending time with God in prayer, being grateful, and counting my blessings. After that, I continue by reading a proverb, praying for loved ones and the world, and then finish by saying my personal affirmations that cover the areas of family, wealth, business, philanthropy, relationships, ministry and health. I repeat this affirmation five times to get it deeper into my spirit and subconscious mind. Next, I look at my dream wall that has strategic pictures for areas I desire to obtain in my life from the spectrum of travel, all the way over to philanthropy. When I have spoken what I expect my life to become, prayed and visualized my future, I feel like I'm armed and ready for my day. To be become truly healthy, I began to see how important it was to nurture the mind body and spirit.

My final area of research that I found to be vital for optimum health was the value of taking cold showers and intermittent fasting. Again, I have to thank Wim Hof for his powerful YouTube videos on the power of cold showers and ice baths. I learned that being in a cold shower for a couple minutes helped dramatically increase circulation making the blood vessels dilate to handle the colder temperature. Taking the showers at first were shocking to my system and I didn't like them. However, as I kept doing them, I felt way more energized and revitalized. There was something powerful about taking me out of my comfort zone.

Stevie (as I began to call him) had ways of challenging me to stay on top of my habit of doing cold showers every morning. I liked the accountability because when I used this before, it always had consistent results.

Finally, I began to do intermittent fasting, which means I gave up eating breakfast and didn't eat until 1:00 in the afternoon. I learned the value of this fast was that it allowed my body to cleanse itself fully and also let my body rest more so it didn't have to work as hard. Science has proven that intermittent fasting will help you live longer, so that sold me. Another benefit was that it slowly began to shed excess pounds as I fasted. The benefits from intermittent fasting were that I felt more rested and had more energy throughout the day. I could feel the positive effects of giving my body more time to cleanse itself.

With all the new changes I have mentioned here, one thing I am more aware of is how sensitive my body has become to what is healthy and unhealthy for my body. When I ate like everyone else, it was like my senses were deadened to how bad the food was for me. Once I went on my first cleanse and came back to the unhealthy and especially high sugar foods, it was as if my body didn't want it anymore. It's like my body had awakened from its slumber.

About the Author

Jimmy Gleason

Jimmy Gleason, professional tennis player, coach, author and inspirational speaker, resides in Laguna Beach, CA. Contact Jimmy at gleasontennis@ yahoo.com or coachjimmyg.com.

Stop Battling Disease and Start Building Wellness

Tonijean Kulpinski

I'm Tonijean Kulpinski, and I am on a God-given mission to help transform the health of this nation and world with the truth revealed in nature's medicine and the connection inside of every human. I learned from my own personal health transformation, going from serious health issues to perfect health, that our bodies have the innate wisdom of self-healing.

Some of the health issues I suffered include migraines, chronic digestive issues, panic attacks, anxiety, mood swings, constant fear, blood glucose intolerance, dizzy spells, kidney stones and gallstones, gallbladder attacks, thyroid issues, hormonal disturbances, severe weight fluctuations, being heavily overweight and extremely underweight, bone loss, and cancer. I suffered from the early age of 16 years old with these chronic health conditions and always felt scared because I was never well. I believe my health issues began as a result of yo-yo dieting to fit into the latest fashion trends. Additionally, I became a hair color specialist at the age of 19, which exposed me to many carcinogenic chemicals.

By the time I was in my mid to late 20s I was a successful salon owner but paid a huge price with my health. I breathed in many caustic chemicals that led to the diagnosis of second stage renal cell carcinoma, also known as kidney cancer. Traces of hair dye were located in my kidney after a biopsy. Fortunately, the cancer was encapsulated, which meant it was nowhere else in my body.

In 2008, I had my left kidney removed by the advice of the medical profession. After the surgery, I still suffered from all of the other health issues that plagued me. I felt my body was a prison and at that point I was completely defeated. I knew somewhere in my heart that just by removing a body part wasn't the answer to preventing the cancer from ever returning.

I cried out to God and asked Him to show me another way that would not only heal my body but prevent it from future illness. God spoke to my heart and told me in a still, small voice to, "Go to Scripture where you will find your answers." He told me that He will heal me if I diligently follow what the Bible explains about healing, because He is using me through this journey for something great.

Although I had peace about the direction God was leading me, I was a bit reluctant to go to the Bible for answers on health and healing. I never thought that the Scriptures would be a manual or a health guide that was the answer that I needed all along. I opened every book of the Bible that pertained to healing and discovered principles and guidelines that I began to follow. These Scriptures were based on food and cleansing that healed my body and mind right from the start.

Initially, I went through a bit of a detox, which typically lasted about two weeks. My body purged all the years of toxicity that caused such havoc on my immune system. Our immune system is our first line of defense against disease. I learned that cancer is a symptom of a compromised immune system and removing the body part that has cancer isn't the answer in preventing it from ever coming back. Through this medical method of "treating" cancer, it will only show its ugly face somewhere else in the body.

The only way to prevent cancer from ever returning is to build immunity by removing the causes and incorporating the cure. Just to name a few of the causes, pesticides are chemical fertilizers that are sprayed on our food which poison and deplete the soil. Depleted soil leads to less nutritious food since our vegetation relies on healthy soil packed with minerals and vitamins. Poor quality water sources, microwaves, processed foods, chemical ridden and hormone laden meat and dairy, toxic skin and hair care products, and deadly emotions such as anger and the inability to forgive compound the assault on our body.

To name a few of the many cures—which by the way have been around longer then the cause—are: cleansing, juicing, and consuming whole, organic foods since organic is the origin of our food and the only way nature intended. The mouth is the organ for the foods we eat and the words we speak that are both responsible for the formation of our cells. Positive words and thoughts lend a hand, as I believe our mouths are the most important organ. We have a choice of what we are made of; our food source and words can be our greatest weapon against disease or can be some of the root causes of illness. Remember, our age and genetics are not prerequisites to disease as we've been led to believe. It is not a mystery why one gets sick. There is always a cause.

I am excited to tell you that by incorporating the principles and guidelines of whole food nutrition, I have lived each and every single day of the last decade of my life while on this journey complete health. I don't have good days and bad days; every day is a good day of health for me. I diligently follow the nutritional and lifestyle commands of the Bible. I thank God every day for directing me on the path of vibrant health and a totally new profession to educate the masses about self-healing. If I had the opportunity to change my past, I would never do that because it is what placed me on the path to self-healing. More importantly, it gave me the opportunity to free others from the bondage of the disease management industry.

I mostly thank God for saving my life so I can be a vessel of truth to those that want to live in extraordinary health. Using both knowledge and wisdom, along with my own personal journey, I wrote this in the hope of changing many lives. I have not even had as little as a cold during the 10 years of my new lifestyle. I don't ever have migraines or any digestive issues. Not a single day of my life goes by that I suffer from any type of sickness. I am 47 years old and I feel as if I am a healthy 20 year old with great energy all the time and sleep peacefully at night.

No one has to suffer; sickness is an opportunity to transform your own health to be a testament to inspire others to do the same. I hope I have inspired you with my personal story and testimony. I believe my greatest credential is not just the documents that hang on the wall of my office, but my life story from very sick to extraordinarily healthy.

I am a graduate of The Institute for Integrative Nutrition, the world's largest nutrition school. I am a Certified Biblical Health Coach and a Board-Certified Holistic Drugless Practitioner. I am also the owner of Heaven on Earth Healing Center, Inc., where I have dedicated my private practice to educating patients how to stop battling disease and start building wellness.

I dedicate my life helping others heal their body so they can reap the blessings of amazing health the way I do. Through my business, I help anyone, no matter what they are suffering from, to maximize their body's ability to heal itself. I offer telephone appointments for those that live out of state or are unable to travel due to sickness, so great health is only a phone call away. Please contact my office by calling (845) 391-8639 to set up your initial telephone or in-office appointment. You can also visit my website at www.Tonijeankulpinski.com. I look forward to working with you on reaching all your nutritional goals successfully.

My book will guide you on the pathway to self-healing by teaching you the causes of sickness from the modern food industry and big Pharma and exactly every aspect of what you need to do to avoid it and build wellness. Sickness is a result of a disconnection of nature and the human body. We need to go back to simplicity by incorporating the wisdom of ancient principles and its reconnection within us. Please keep in mind, in order to completely heal your body, you must remove the causes because the body doesn't have any room for these toxic interferences that inhibit your bodies potential to heal. You cannot totally heal the body only by adding good food but still consuming the bad stuff.

Unlock your God-given health potential by reading my life changing, best-selling book. You will learn about topics such as:

- Organic verses non organic foods
- Biblical principles
- Marketing strategies
- Healing modalities
- Detoxing
- Earthing and grounding
- Juicing & blending
- Superfoods
- The best and worst water sources
- Proper rest and sleep
- The truth about supplements
- The meat and dairy industry
- Grains
- Gluten
- Fish farming
- The different types of eggs
- Meal plans
- Recipes
- Cookware
- Fats and oils
- The cholesterol myth
- Spices and sweeteners
- The dangers of refined salt and the many benefits of real, unrefined salt
- The truth behind coffee and tea
- Non-dairy milks
- The dangers of soy

I also include a resource section to guide you of the best of my suggestions on everything from rebounders, to food products, cookware, hair and skin care, dish and clothes detergent, cleaning products, and so much more. To pick up your copy of my best-selling book please go to Amazon.com and search for *Stop Battling Disease and Start Building Wellness* now, your guide to extraordinary health.

About the Author

Tonijean Kulpulski

Tonijean Kulpinski is a board certified Holistic Practitioner, a certified Biblical Health Coach, a member of The American Association of Drugless Practitioners and The Weston A. Price Foundation. Tonijean is the owner of her private practice, Heaven On Earth Healing Center, Inc. where she educates her clients how to build wellness in their bodies through self love and whole food nutrition. Shes has made several television appearances on TBN'S *Joy in Our Town* and *Doctor To Doctor*, televised from The Manhattan Studio. In addition to the show, *Book Talk* and *The Victorious Life Show*.

Tonijean is a graduate of The Institute for Integrative Nutrition, the world's largest nutrition school. She is also a graduate of The Biblical Health Institute founded by a Jordan S. Rubin. Tonijean teaches holistic nutrition at The Desmond Campus of Mount Saint Mary's College for adult enrichment. She bases her teachings on raw, whole, superfood nutrition, and guidelines and principles that are stated clearly in scripture. Tonijean is a published author of the best selling book *Stop Battling Disease and Start Building Wellness.* She believes in eating food only in the form God created. Toni is a public speaker and gives holistic nutrition seminars around the country and in her surrounding areas based on these principles. She has learned from her own, personal health experience that food in the form God created is the medicine that heals.

Solving the "Always Tired" Syndrome

Ed Strachar

Feeling tired often is a common complaint. Chronic Fatigue Syndrome plagues millions of people worldwide, and supposedly there is no cure. Supposedly? Pay attention and you will know there is one and may even be able to implement it.

Even if you have plenty of energy, you can have more. Who would choose to turn it down? You have to remember that infinite energy/power is all around us. If it's not flowing through you, it's because it's all blocked up and/or its being stolen/usurped by energy thieves. If you are often tired when you shouldn't be, then this is probably what is going on. The solution, very simply, is to clear the blockages and get rid of the thieves. Good nutrition, supplements, physical exercise, yoga, organic food all for the most part are great practices, yet they will not accomplish the task themselves. Things like forgiveness and kindness can help. Forgiveness will unblock the heart as it is the center of your energy body. That is a key point of understanding.

Thus, "heart" exercises can make a huge difference. Kindness will expand the heart as does gratitude; all can release some blockages yet heavier ones will require more power.

According to the HeartMath Institute, the heart is 100,000 times the strength of the brain electrically and 5,000 times more powerful magnetically. That is huge! Because of this, nutrition is clearly not the answer, nor is positive thinking and visualization. Those are mental activities. The brain is center of the nervous system. The energy system is our concern here.

A deeper understanding of higher energy and how to use it to build your own energy is where you can solve the "always tired syndrome." Clearing deeper blockages such as pent up negative emotion, negative memories, heartache, trauma, rejection, family issues/conflict and relationship strife takes more work at higher, more powerful dimensions and is often a large cause of deeper blockages to our energy. Unchecked, this alone can greatly weaken us and make one then susceptible to disease and can sometimes be fatal. This is why you hear about stories of forgiveness of resolution of a conflict when someone is supposedly on their death bed and soon recover. The blockage in effect was removed, and just like a cleared drain, things flowed again and health was restored.

What about the Energy Thieves?

Probably the least understood and most uncomfortable to discuss for most people including professionals in this field is the aspect of energy thieves. I will call them "evil." Evil comes in the form for evil spirits, evil entities, demons, witchcraft, black magic, sorcery, negative soul contracts, false angels, and spirit guides, to name a few. These are hidden, usually invisible to the naked eye. You see evidence of them in horror movies, yet many think it's only fiction. It is not. These entities cannot live off the cosmic vibration of the universe. Instead, the need to, simply put, get their energy off those that do.

Over 95 percent of the people who come to me with an issue have some form of evil; most have no idea. Physicians and medical professionals are usually totally clueless about them. I am not. For me personally, I was weighed down with so much of this and had no idea about them. I felt I was a good person and reasonably kind, helped people, gave to charity, and was very religious, being a Born Again Christian for 20 years.

Well, I had to wake up and learn. I was very naive about the real truth about the spirit world. In my case, everything started going wrong. My head was bombarded with negative imagery that would prevent me from working effectively. Many of my business dealings would fall through for no apparent reason and yet I had no idea what was really happening. I prayed with many great and sincere pastors over the Bible to no significant effect.

It wasn't until one of my greatest teachers, Raymon Grace, not only exposed me to them but also had the power to clear them. Most healers simply lack the power to do this, and many healers don't even acknowledge or understand them. For me, it was a question of figuring this out or ending my life. I was very close to doing just that.

I have had many clients come to me, telling me of all the previous healers they have been to with only short term, slightly positive effects at best until they work with me. I am strict, serious, and determined as dealing with this evil is serious business. Most healers are weak, sick and broken themselves. This is mostly because they don't know how to handle this side of the spiritual spectrum nor have the power to effectively do so. What happens to them is a negative energy field is created around them that repels what they want and attracts what they don't want. This is the effect of evil and often what people call bad luck. Thus, I am continuously cleaning my energy and a raising my power and vibrations which makes it much more difficult to be vulnerable to attack. I teach people how to do this themselves in my online www.SelfHealingMastery.net course.

In summary, to solve the always tired/chronic fatigue issue, we need to connect to the infinite energy and clear the blockages and thieves! Do this and you can be highly energized and much more effective at anything you do in life. Higher energy always attracts. These principles have healed a wide range of conditions including depression, bad luck, constant failure, failed organs, disease, cancer, and a host of other conditions.

Raising One's Energy and Vibrations: The Power of Pyramids

We all know the great Pyramids in Giza, Egypt. Some think it's a mystery who built them. Let me tell you, it's no mystery.

Instead, it is hidden knowledge as the ones who know don't want you to know. If you did find out, the dark power structures of energy/fossil fuels, religions, and government would come crashing down faster than a lead balloon in a lightning storm.

These pyramids are aligned precisely to North, South, East and West to within .1 degree of accuracy. Furthermore, their height is the exact average height across the earth at that longitudinal line. Even more fascinating is the fact that the speed of light is precisely 299,722,458 meters per second. The exact pyramid coordinates are -29.9722458 degrees North.

This is all fascinating and the deeper knowledge can fill many volumes, but we won't go into that here. I will tell you that pyramids saved my life. What's important to know is that pyramids are both energy generators and energy magnifiers. (Pyro = fire, mid = middle, pyramid means fire in the middle.) This has to do with their special geometry and the way the cosmic vibrations of matter in the universal energy field work.

To Elaborate, in David Wilcock's brilliant book, *Source Field Investigations*, he discusses pyramids at length. Fascinating experiments were conducted in Russia where pyramids were placed over polluted water and the water became purified! They took dead seeds; ones that were burned in a fire, placed them inside a pyramid. The seeds sprouted after several days, so clearly they had some life-giving and purification power. This was what was important for me to know. So how did they save my life? I'll explain.

Once or twice a year, I do a detox and cleanse. As I was doing this, the therapist I was working with told me my prostate gland was very large. This was alarming for obvious reasons. At the time, I had about $25 to my name and was living in my mother's spare bedroom and was in a very bad place both spiritually and emotionally. The herbs for prostate issues in the health food store cost over $30. It was the only non-medical solution I knew. A simple doctor's appointment would have cost me hundreds of dollars that I did not have.

So I had to think a bit. Remembering what David Wilcock shared about pyramids and what I know about energy projection, I projected myself into the giant pyramids in Giza. Projection is a very powerful energy tool if done correctly. It is where, using over 99 percent heart energy but 1 percent or less imagination, you "project" the image with energy. This must be done with a still mind for best results. Doing this correctly can give you the same if not better effect as being in a physical pyramid. (It's obviously a lot easier and less expensive.) This is not visualization; that is done solely with the imagination, has much less power, and thus effectiveness.

I also projected a smaller pyramid about the size of a football around my prostate area. In conjunction, I asked and saw my prostate reducing to normal and had a ton of gratitude in my heart for doing so. As I did so, I could feel the magnetic field I created. It was profound. I did this several times over the next few days.

When I returned to the therapist about a week later, she made a point to tell me that my prostate amazingly had returned to normal size! This led me to some profound healing breakthroughs with people in both using pyramids and teaching people to project and direct energy and connect to the universal cosmic vibration. Mastering the skills of clearing and opening your heart wider, connecting to the infinite heart of the Universe, combined with raising your vibrations and energy using the power of pyramids can lead to some fascinating breakthroughs in self-healing, energizing, and more.

About the Author

Ed Strachar

In my Healing Genius YouTube channel, there are free exercises that guide this. One is called the Love Expansion Energy Healing Exercise. The www.SelfHealingMastery.net course is a very comprehensive training involving these exercises and many, many more.
www.HealingGenius.com, Facebook.com/EdStracharSpiritHealer

Awakening in Body, Mind, and Spirit

Cameron Cushing

This is a story about changing my diet, which altered my thoughts and ultimately led to transforming my life and reality as I once knew it. Back in early 2006 a student at my workplace had placed a documentary on my desk titled "Eating", about factory farming in Canada. Prior to this, I had not considered what type of life animals experience before ending up wrapped in plastic and sold in a grocery store. Something else I had not considered was the possibility that animals are artificially bred and treated as a commodity for profit.

I watched the video that evening and was horrified with what I saw. I felt a disconnect between the deep love I have always had for animals and what I was led to believe was good to eat and actually healthy for us. Needless to say, I chose to stop eating animals the very next day. Here begins my journey of unlearning the lies I had been taught about food and a whole lot more, and relearning what it means to be healthy, happy and in love with myself and life.

Your body is your temple; we only get one body in this

lifetime. Get present to that statement because it's a universal truth. Have you ever asked yourself why it appears like the masses are treating their bodies as a garbage can? Much of what people consume daily is not being eliminated and literally eats away at us from the inside out. Did you ever stop to think that maybe there is a hidden agenda behind all the money "they" keep spending on marketing to advertise/hypnotize us with "their" truths as to what we need to eat to stay healthy?

If you were to fill up your gas tank with coca cola and replace your motor oil with cow's milk, how far do you think you would get before your vehicle stopped working? Why is it then that people so willingly consume highly acidic sodas and drink milk from an animal's teats? Is it possible that there are dark forces at play brainwashing you? I wonder why schools have not yet implemented a curriculum that teaches us all about the basic fundamentals of living life powerfully and living a life you love? Human sickness and dis-ease is a vicious cycle and the largest epidemic in today's society. A large percentage of the food I was eating on a daily basis as a child (and well into adulthood), was dead and processed in some way, shape, or form. Our bodies are electric and so it makes sense that living, whole foods are a match for the electric body. We are the only species on earth that cooks our food and we are the most confused when it comes to eating right for optimal health. For example, we have been misled to believe that cooking the dead rotting flesh of a diseased animal and gorging it down for about ten minutes of pleasure is not only good for us, but necessary for health reasons like, "we need protein." Just because something tastes good doesn't mean it is good for you. By the way, your body does not need protein. Your body needs amino acids, the simple form of protein found in every living whole food grown on earth. The only reason I ate meat was because it tasted good and I was taught that it was good for me.

You can trick your body into believing anything is good for it if you do it for long enough. For example, if you can teach your body to become addicted to cigarettes (which I did in high school), alcohol and poor food choices, this means you can also teach your body to want whole foods that will actually make you feel good long term. If you truly desire to improve your physical health, I can suggest a few simple changes that over time will produce profound lasting results. Start by eating whole, organic foods daily. Organic is the way nature intended it. Feed your body fruits, hearty salads and vegetables a minimum of once a day. Incorporating sprouts, herbs, nuts, seeds, and legumes into your diet several times a week will give you ample energy and have you feeling very satisfied. The more you develop this habit of eating healthy, whole foods, the more your body will thank you in ways you haven't yet imagined. Cooking food kills the living enzymes found in them and depreciates the nutritional benefits so the more uncooked food you eat the better it will be for you.

There are so many great books and educational programs out there that will teach you how to eat right and make it taste amazing, so take some time and educate yourself from people who walk their talk. However, your body is ultimately your best teacher, so don't overload yourself with information. If you just start with one month of eating natural whole foods daily, I guarantee you will have more energy and feel absolutely amazing.

Your body is a living being so doesn't it make sense to eat foods that are fresh and living? If you smoke, stop it right now. You are unconsciously attempting to kill yourself every time you inhale a cigarette. Pay attention to the dialogue going on in your head and if you don't like something about yourself then change it. All success or failure begins with a person's self-talk and self-thought. If you drink alcohol, reduce your consumption to 1 to 4 drinks a month, on social occasions only, and preferably only drink craft beer or red wine. Alcohol is poison, and there is a very good reason that "they" don't want us to know why alcohol and cigarettes were legalized in the first place (and why a medicinal plant like marijuana was criminalized almost 100 years ago). Daily exercise is key to longevity. The human body is meant to move. The simple act of stretching and taking a brisk walk 20-30 minutes a day will make a world of difference long term. Muscle mass depreciates as we age, so incorporating weekly strength training of some sort will keep your muscles visible and help prevent unforeseen future problems in the body.

Lastly, and definitely very important, is drink properly cleaned water. The best times to drink water are the moment you wake up, a minimum of 30 minutes before you eat a meal, at least 90 minutes after eating a meal and periodically throughout the day. Any fluids you consume less than 30 minutes before, during or up to 90 minutes after a meal will flush enzymes out of your stomach, making it harder for your body to digest food. Your body is made up of approximately 80 percent salt water, so drinking an average of one ounce of clean water for every two pounds of body weight daily is a standard guideline to follow. Good physical health consists of 85 percent food intake and 15 percent exercise on a daily basis. You are what you eat so eat well. Total health is a combination of the foods you eat, the air you breathe, the thoughts you think, and the actions you take!

Over time as I changed my diet, my thoughts started to change with little to no effort. I started to notice a big difference in the reduction of negative thinking and the addition of positive thoughts. When we remove something from our life that no longer serves us, space is created for something new to come in and take its place. The more I started to feel better from what I was eating and the more my body started to change and appreciate the foods I was consuming, the better I felt in body and mind. Thought is a powerful form of physical and emotional manifestation and when we change the way we think, the world around us transforms. To live a healthy, vibrant life means one must create harmony within body, mind, and spirit. Detoxing your body of all that which is not nourishing you will remove toxicity, eliminate stored fat (acid waste), prevent sickness, reverse aging, prolong lifespan, eliminate the possibility of unnatural death, promote self-care, clear negative thinking from the mind, and provide a clear space for you to connect with your higher spiritual self. That statement alone should be inspiration enough for you to change your life in a way that offers you more joy and greater purpose.

One of the things you have control over in life is the thoughts you choose, so why not recondition your mind to use powerful words as a way to speak about yourself and others, your life, and what you are up to in the world? The power that comes from using positive words as a way of speaking is unlimited. The very simple act of removing a few negative words like *can't, try, should,* and *hate* from your language and replacing them with *I can, I am, I will* and *I love* will reshape your posture and outlook on life. Positive words and phrases feel good, uplift the human spirit and have people around you smiling with a genuine sense of happiness. Once I became aware of how I was diminishing myself and others with the words I used, the choice to change my words by eliminating negative ones and replacing them with positive ones became easy and fun. Words have immense power and they carry a vibration that sends a direct message out to the universe.

I know in my heart that everyone on this earth has the desire, ability and will power to choose happiness over any other state of being. I am living proof that positive speaking creates a higher vibration and transforms life. Thoughts create feelings and when we feel thoughts that empower us, we have the ability to inspire, uplift and empower others. If you change the way you think inside, the world around you will change. Words literally create worlds, so choose them wisely because the words you speak tell the story of who you are now and who you are to become. Simple living and higher thinking produces great happiness.

This leads to my newfound connection with spirit. I refer to spirit as that all knowing, all encompassing, *I am energy* that resides within every living being (and yes, that includes *you*). As I started to cleanse my body by removing a large percentage of what I had been eating and replacing my intake with more wholesome living foods, I immediately started to feel better physically. As I started to feel better in my body, my mind and thought energy started to shift with very little effort on my part. As I started to notice that my negative thought patterns were disappearing, I began to make conscious choices to teach myself how to generate more positivity in my day-to-day life. This is where daily living really started to become enjoyable. When a negative thought arose, I would catch it in the act, thank it for sharing, and remind myself that negativity no longer resides here. Spirit, the higher self, is our personal guide that works hand-in-hand with you and serves as your intuition. Spirit has no judgment and is not responsible for choosing the actions or outcomes we carry fourth in the physical world. Spirit just is, a subtle guide so to speak, and all one has to do is slow down and listen. Spirit is and always has been right there with you.

One of the greatest experiences for me with reconnecting to my higher non-judgmental spirit self was the realization that life in the physical world actually begins and ends in spirit. There is no birth or death in spirit and we are all one energy choosing to be here in physical form. We are the watcher and witness to all life has to offer in the physical world. Once I realized this, I started to become the observer of every aspect of my life. Here is what I mean by becoming the observer of my life: I no longer suppress my feelings, I do not act out in aggression towards others, and I do not become attached to the sensations that arise and pass in my physical body. When being in a state of observation, judgment ceases to exist. With an understanding that life is impermanent, ever changing, and flows with no beginning or end, one can now observe what happens in the body and physical surroundings without reacting. I reflect on is what happening without reacting and take right action only after consideration, moving forward with a knowing that I feel good about my actions.

Knowing that I attract every experience I have allows me the ability to live my life with integrity and take full responsibility for the world in which I create. You can either play the victim in life (everything happens to me) or you can be the writer, director, and lead role of your movie (I create and take full responsibility for my experience). "I am the creator of my reality" is one of the most powerful and profound statements I choose to live by. Does my humanness or animal instinct get in the way from time to time? Absolutely. In the heat of the moment do I occasionally want to crush people for their unconscious thoughtless acts? Yeah, I do.

However, wisdom is knowing that change cannot be made

by feeding into the very problem that arises in the first place. As a man of integrity, I know that I all-ways need to choose to the best of my ability to walk a higher ground. Mistakes made are opportunities for growth and it is my belief that without them, we would live a pretty dull existence on earth. I no longer say sorry for my mistakes because sorry has no power. I apologize when necessary and make new promises to others in the face of my mistakes. To live a healthy vibrant life is to live a life in harmony with body, mind, and spirit.

Your body is the vessel you have to move around with in this world, so honoring and respecting your body is paramount. I honor my body daily by giving it clean water, wholesome foods, physical exercise, positive thinking, prayer, meditation, and gratitude for all that is now and all that is coming towards me. I take time every day to connect with nature, plants, and animals. I believe that nature keeps living and plants keep growing in order to provide for the environment and all sentient beings on earth. Animals are our friends and they are here to teach us about love, honor, and personal boundaries. Humans are here for the experience of emotion, conscious expansion, and mostly to be in a constant state of love and service to others. We share this world together as one and we deserve to live a life of peace, joy and equanimity. All for one and one for all.

About the Author

Cameron Cushing

Cameron Cushing is a Transformational Coach and Mentor. His gift to you is authentic self-expression. He is a natural teacher, a deliverer of a message, a 'channel' for information to be expressed into the world around us. His fundamental teachings are based on language and self-empowerment. Cameron is an expert at communication. His powerful gift is using language as a transformational tool to introduce others to new ways of looking at life, truly helping others to change at the level of thought and mind. He uses words and language as the messenger to pass on a mental thought or concept into the minds of whomever he is talking to. It's completely innate within him to move and inspire people into taking action through words. Cameron is a natural channel for wisdom that comes to him in the present moment through writing, coaching, mentorship, and public speaking.

To Contact Cameron for coaching, mentorship, public speaking engagements, or to elaborate on anything he has written about here, please email training@ cameroncushing.com or visit www.cameroncushing.com

What is Vibrant Health?

Dr. Shan Hussain

How would you personally envisage vibrant health?

And what would this kind of health mean for you?

I believe the subject of health is very simple, but many people seem to make it complicated. I can't speculate on their reasons why, but as a medical doctor I've seen incredible changes in the delivery of health care over the last two decades. Doctors are instructed to change the recommendations we give whenever new evidence arises, and it's reached the point where the half-life of our medical knowledge is now thought to be only seven years.

Back in 1994, the dean of my medical school warned us this would happen. At our very first lecture, we sat in a cold autumnal theatre when he announced, "By the time you all become doctors, half of everything I'm about to teach you today will be wrong. The problem is, I just don't know which half…"

This declaration was both amusing and frightening. But health information is now more abundant than ever. It is estimated that over 80 percent of all knowledge is now freely available on the Internet, yet so much of it is conflicting.

But somewhere in the midst of all his, surely there are some basic health principles that can withstand the test of time?

In 1948, the World Health Organisation (WHO) defined health as "a state of complete physical, mental and social well-being, not merely the absence of disease or infirmity." I recall hearing this definition in school and looking around the room, wondering if anyone could ever claim to have this kind of health. It was an enlightening moment when I realized that being free from illness does not equal health. And understanding this concept changed the way I looked at health forever.

We all have different images of health. Some of us might equate health to having six-pack abdominals or maybe only 10 percent body fat. Others may say that health is an inner feeling of strength, joy, and well-being. Some might even feel that being healthy just means having the ability to survive each day.

But it's important to remember that health is a tool, not an outcome. So my bigger question is this: What would vibrant health mean for you personally? How would it improve your energy levels, your appearance, your relationships, your job, your income, your confidence, your self-image, your social standing or your future?

If you're not sure, try completing the following sentence:
"With vibrant health, I would be able to _____."

The WHO's powerful definition of health has remained unchallenged for the last 70 years. And we can break this definition down further:

- Complete physical well-being (the body)
- Complete mental well-being (the mind)
- Complete social well-being (the environment)

Now it is absolutely vital that these three areas are kept in balance. If we really think about it, practically every non-genetic illness can be traced back to an imbalance in one's physical, mental, or social well-being. Something I've noticed working, as a doctor over the last two decades is that physical, mental, or social imbalance is the fundamental basis of most, if not all disease.

It is scientifically proven that type 2 diabetes, heart disease, depression, anxiety, stroke, obesity, hypertension, and even some cancers all have preventable elements to them. So how do we prevent these conditions? Simple—by ensuring that our physical, mental, and social health are all kept in balance.

If we balance these three areas and work on improving each of them, by definition we move towards achieving better health. But if we ignore, neglect, or fail to address an imbalance in one or more of these areas, we move towards illness.

My interest in holistic health first began by trying to determine what actually causes people to develop this imbalance. Why do people fall ill? As I came back to this definition, the answer was in fact very simple—stress. Physical, mental, or social stress moves people away from health and toward illness.

But if we work together and really address these three areas with sufficient focus and attention, we can actually reverse stress and move people towards health very quickly. What I discovered is if we recognize and identify stress early, we can actually prevent a huge amount of illness.

Identifying such people and finding where their health is out of balance is my area of expertise. In my work as a health and wellness advisor, I've managed to simplify these areas of health using three very basic principles: The three principles of enduring health.

Principle #1: What we put in to and what we eliminate from our physical body determines the state of our physical health.

Your body has an estimated 40 trillion cells that constantly renew themselves. For example, your skin is only 2-4 weeks old. Your red blood cells are less than 120 days old, and your liver fully regenerates itself every five months. So think of the human body not as a rigid structure, but as a fluid system in constant regeneration. How do we support this we regeneration? We need to make sure we feed ourselves with good quality nutrients and ensure we allow our bodies to eliminate the waste products that our cells constantly create.

There are only eight essential components to the human diet, and this is where we get the raw materials needed to support this constant regeneration:

1. Carbohydrates
2. Proteins
3. Fats
4. Minerals
5. Vitamins
6. Fiber
7. Water
8. Oxygen

But here's the problem: Despite a tremendous amount of research, we still don't know the exact amount of these components we need to consume every single day. There are various guidelines and recommendations, but these are not precise or specific to you and your constitution. However, what is clear is that if there is an imbalance in our intake of any of these components, we risk moving towards illness.

For example, a diet rich in carbohydrates can make us feel tired and moody. It also puts us at risk of developing Type 2 diabetes, obesity, and cardiovascular disease. If we don't consume enough water, we are at risk of dehydration, headaches, lethargy, weight gain, and recurrent infections. If we don't consume enough fiber, we are at risk of mood changes, constipation, diverticular disease, bowel cancer, and even cardiovascular disease. That is why it is vital that we address any imbalance in our intake of these components to help support the constant regeneration of our cells.

Also essential is that our bodies are allowed to eliminate the waste products our cells create from their daily functions. There are only four main elimination channels:

1. Bowels
2. Urinary tract
3. Skin
4. Lungs

Promoting elimination from these channels every day helps to prevent waste matter building up in our bodies. To encourage this elimination, I advise people to ensure they have plenty of water, fiber, activity, perspiration, skin stimulation, and deep breathing exercises. Something I have noted with my clients is if they just focus on supporting elimination channels that encourage the passing of this waste matter; it can have an incredible effect on their energy levels and weight loss.

We also need to make sure our bodies have sufficient levels of activity and rest. (After all, we live in cycles of activity and rest.) The human body is designed to be active, and numerous studies back up the fact that we must take regular amounts of daily activity. Amongst many benefits, this can have remarkable effects on our energy, mood, and immunity levels.

Just as importantly, we need to ensure we take sufficient levels of physical and mental rest to allow the body to heal, recover, and regenerate. Common sense and countless studies tell us that if there is a sustained imbalance in our levels of activity and rest, this creates physical stress on our bodies, which can show up as illness.

Principle #2: Our thoughts, feelings and emotions, and how we manage them will determine the state of our mental and emotional well-being.

Dr. Deepak Chopra wrote an excellent book called *Quantum Healing*, where he describes that a human being has an average of 60,000 thoughts per day. Surprisingly, 95% of those thoughts are repeated the following day. But despite the research, scientists still do not fully understand exactly where human thought comes from. What is clear though is our ability to decide how we want to react to a thought. We can consciously choose thoughts and direct them to feelings and emotions that will serve us, and we can always decide on a better meaning that we want to attach to our thoughts.

Why is this so important? Because the thoughts we have, and the feelings and emotions they trigger can have a profound physiological effect on the health of your body. When people constantly embrace stressful, worrying, upsetting thoughts, the body can create certain hormones, neurotransmitters, and biochemical responses that in the long run can be harmful. While this has been proven scientifically, it is also very logical. But on the flip side, if we focus our thoughts on feelings such as gratitude, love, pride, and joy, the body creates hormones and neurotransmitters such as dopamine, serotonin, and endorphins, which have powerful and supportive effects on our health. It is therefore vital to make sure that we are able to manage our thoughts and control our perceptions at any given time.

Principle #3: How (and who) we interact with in our environment determines the state of our social health.

There's an old saying that goes "You are what you eat." I would extend that by saying "you are what you consume." Anything that you absorb from your environment has the potential ability to affect your health. This can include the news, television, books, magazines, social media, the internet, and most importantly, the people you spend time with.

We can absorb an incredible amount unconsciously from the environment we are placed in. It is therefore so important to ensure that anything we come into contact with in our environment is supportive of our health and well being. As any biology student will tell you, we are the sum of our genes and our environment. While we cannot easily change our genes, we all have the ability to amend our environmental interactions.

Jim Rohn famously said, "You are the average of the five people you spend most time with." So if you want to find a quick way to get vibrant health, simply find five people whose health you want to emulate and spend as much time with them as possible. The point he makes is that whether you like it or not, other people's behavior will rub off on you if you spend sufficient time with them. Again, this is very logical. If we have children that are at school, one of our biggest concerns is that they don't end up "falling into the wrong crowd." Why is that? Surely we should also pay equal attention to the crowd we have fallen into. In my experience, very few people are totally impervious to the company they choose to keep.

I believe that social health is probably the single most powerful influence on our well-being in general, and I predict this area will soon get the widespread attention it deserves. Never lose sight of how your environment can influence your health. If you can't change your environment to one that is more supportive of your health, at least be conscious of how it can influence you. Keep as much of it geared towards health as you can. Decide what and who gets in to your environment. Additionally, consider what and who you should let go. Remember, anything can influence you if you let it.

That was a brief introduction to the three principles, but before we move on, I want to ask a simple question—and that is *why*? Why do you specifically want vibrant health?

One of the first exercises I do with my clients is I ask them to write down 100 reasons why they want to have better health, and I strongly encourage you to do this too. This can take some time, but it's also a very valuable exercise. It really gets the brain thinking to ultimately come up with a number of truly compelling reasons that will help them move towards health.

A few common examples from past clients include:

- having greater energy
- losing excess weight
- getting into the best shape of my life
- being a shining example to others
- being more successful in business
- feeling more confident
- enjoying many more years
- helping more people in my community
- sleeping better
- appearing better
- being respected among my peers

Remember that health is a tool, not an outcome. Never lose sight of your own personal reasons why you want to be healthy. If you have clear, strong, compelling reasons in place that you reflect upon every single day, it is almost inevitable that you will move towards becoming a much healthier and more vibrant person. If you feel like sharing your reasons why, feel free to send them over to me as I would genuinely love to read them.

I believe anyone can use these three principles to their advantage and reclaim vibrant health very quickly. It's worth remembering that doctors are not experts in health, but rather experts in illness. Health is not the absence of disease, and few doctors can genuinely claim to have the ability to heal illness.

In truth, no doctor on the planet can scientifically explain why a broken bone mends, why a wound heals, or why the body clears so many infections by itself. They can describe the stages of healing in microscopic detail. They can use a lot of big words to confuse you, or try to sound clever. But they can't explain why healing happens.

The answer to this question lies in understanding these two simple steps to healing anything:

1. Create and sustain the optimal conditions to enable healing.
2. Allow nature to take its course.

It is my genuine hope that the three principles I have shared here will help you with the first step. Always remember that vibrant health does not start with our doctor; it starts with us and the choices we make.

About the Author

Dr. Shan Hussain

Dr. Shan has been a medical doctor for 18 years. He graduated from Imperial College in London, England and spent his first 7 years as a doctor working in hospital medicine. He has been a General Practitioner for the last 11 years and has developed a special interest in health promotion and disease prevention. He also has training in neurolinguistic programming, a diploma, with distinction, in coaching, and certification in healing. He is the no.1 best-selling author of the book, *The Big Prescription.* which is available through Amazon. His consulting work is focused on helping individuals, business leaders, and corporations eliminate the debilitating effects of stress through groundbreaking wellness programs. As a result, not only does individual health improve, but so does well-being, energy, vitality and performance.

Doctor, Author, Health and Wellness Advisor, Healer
Linkedin : www.linkedin.com/in/dr-shan-hussain
Facebook : www.facebook.com/drshanhussain
Instagram : @dr.shanhussain
Twitter : @drshanhussain
Email : enquiries@thehealthstudio.net
www.shanhussain.com
www.thehealthstudio.net

Ignite the Fire Within You!
Celebrate a Healthy Vibrant Life

Steve Olson

As a product of our human society we are truly blessed with a unique DNA that encompasses innate values that are exclusive to us, which can never be duplicated. Not one of us should try to be someone else, simply because it's not achievable and is not going to happen. Simply stated, "who we are, can only be, who we are!" Pressures and expectations of others do not define us. Our true character comes from within ourselves and fulfillment rises from the calling each of us pursues.

We are who we are. The actions we take are stronger than our words. As one wise sage emphatically shares, "If you can see it and believe it, you can achieve it." Our minds are powerful tools we are born with. Many of us have the opportunity to build, nourish and grow our own pathways. What makes the difference is relishing your own personal journey, not those that are not yours. Attempting to emulate what society and others expect, usually leads to a frustrating life of boredom and dissatisfaction.

Embrace who you are, not who you think you should be.

Today our evolving world, at times, may create challenges and uneasiness that can complicate our not so simple lives. It's not uncommon to periodically question ourselves, what we are doing, where we are headed, and what our end-game plan should look like.

There may be times we are frustrated and not happy with the role we think we should be playing. This fantasy of envy is not healthy or productive, yet at times might cloud our thoughts. It's unfortunate. We need to resist the trappings of our society that lure us to look outward rather than inward.

As Popeye, the children's cartoon character always reminds us, "I am what I am!" All of us have our attributes as well as our shortcoming. Personally, I have been blessed with the opportunity to be successful as a consulting executive for multiple large and emerging companies. Yet my competencies in other business arenas falls short. Put me in the role of Chief Operating or Financial Officer? Not a chance! I would be asked to pack up and leave the office after the first day on the job.

Take action and separate the dreamers from the doers.

Many people in our awesome beautiful world are simply dreamers. They have fantasies and whimsy' about how they can make a bushel of money creating a revolutionary flying machine in their minds. The problem isn't that it can't happen; the problem is they never take action. The biggest step they take is getting up from their TV set to crack open another can of Budweiser.

Today, our evolving world creates challenges and at times uneasiness can complicate our lives. It's not uncommon to periodically question ourselves, what we are doing, where we are headed, and what our endgame plan should look like. There may be periods where we are frustrated and unhappy with the role we think we should play. There may be a tendency for some to envy others, wishing to emulate living the life of our friends, business colleagues, and others they highly admire.

As an executive advisor for multiple large and emerging companies, I knew I improved the leadership, marketing and sales development skills for these corporations. This was my calling and talent as business performance specialist.

Believe in your own power and avoid the critics

I am always fascinated by negativity and those who cross their arms and exclaim something can't be done. These are not the people you want in your circle of peers. They prefer focusing on the darkness rather than the light, attempting to lure you into their world of negativity.

At the age of 20, I decided to start a jingle business. Many scoffed and asked why I would be so foolish to consider such a fantasy, especially in the competitive New York City market. I'll never forget one individual who rudely rolled his eyes, exclaiming, "Give it up! What you are trying to do just won't work." My thought simply was why not try? I ignored the non-believers and refused to let others take me down.

We all have the gift to believe in ourselves. So moving forward, I took action to start my commercial jingle business. I knocked on doors, sent demos, and eventually built a rewarding part-time business.

At age 30, I left corporate America and started my own marketing agency and other business endeavors. My mother was so worried when I quit my well-paying job to sell door-to-door coupons to local merchants. But then she realized that each of us has the choice to bring greater health and wealth into our lives. We are all unique. When a new door opens, we have the opportunity to embrace our own future; not for those who surround us, but for our own benefit.

Overcome fear and your life can prosper.

A wise friend of mine once told me that without experiencing failure, we can never reach our full potential. Success cannot be achieved without some stumbles along the way. Luck may help us a few times, but it's rare. Reality requires us to carefully plan, test, and evaluate every factor that impacts the ability to achieve our goals. We must have the constitution, relentlessness, and dedication to follow through and hone our personal leadership abilities. If we fear failure, we cannot succeed. If we are too risk averse, we cannot fulfill the talents that lie within ourselves.

You may be surprised to hear this, that many successful

people experience failure before they can realize their goals and achievements. As kids, many of us had to touch the hot stove before we learned not to. Taking calculated chances often provides opportunities for success. If we aren't confident in ourselves, it inhibits our growth and opportunity for a healthy life. If we don't take chances and only travel the safe path, we miss the experiences and joy of personal growth. Taking risks to explore our options can pay off, opening new doors to explore. When it comes right down to it, we are the ultimate safety net for our lives.

Managing productive home lives is the fruit for happy living.

The business of running our home lives at times is not addressed when we consider the needs, wants, and complexities that help make up today's family unit. There are three elements that can make for a happy home. Interestingly enough, the principles of creating a successful family unit requires the same attention that thriving businesses require from their employees. Whether you are at home or work the following three actionable responsibilities can make for a more efficient, effective, and harmonious living environment:

All of us must step up to make our contributions. Each family member must be accountable for their assigned responsibilities. As an example, if young Joe doesn't want to complete his morning chores of picking up and sweeping the outdoor front porch, he has not lived up to his promise.

If Dad did not pick up the cake for Joe's birthday, Mom and Joe will be furious.

However, when Dad puts a sticky note on his car visor reminding him to pick up Joe's cake at the bakery, the entire family celebrates how each one took responsibility to honor their family chores and celebrate their contributions.

Think big and you can accomplish what you really want.

I always remember a conversation with a tennis buddy of mine. He absolutely viewed the world with fascination and a real gusto for life. Happily married, he truly enjoyed his regimented daily life, which was for the most part the same routine every day. He was perfectly content with his repetitious, carefully planned, and predictable schedule. What many considered boring and monotonous was the joy of his daily world.

Bill was quite successful and a true gentleman among his close circle of friends. During his early years, he frequently traveled overseas, living out of his suitcase for months before returning to his Newport Beach waterfront home. He enjoyed his career and achieved success according to his standards. Bill had the ability to enjoy multiple vacations with his wife and friends. Locally, he expanded his new circle of friends into what I now call his "second career." However, Bill was still involved on the sidelines, skyping his overseas colleagues.

He was right where he wanted to be. Bill said to me, "In my world, I'm enjoying life to its fullest on my own terms and my own time." He relished the ultimate stage of his own journey and loved every day of it. Everyone loved Bill and his wife, an awesome couple in total control of their wants, needs, and mission in life. Never underestimate the personal power of connections. Surround your circle of friends with like-minded people.

Several years ago, the health and fitness guru Stevene introduced me to international author and speaker, Harvey Mackay. I was extremely excited to have this opportunity, as his Best Seller, *Swim with Sharks,* was an unusually insightful book that had a profound impact on my business success. I asked Harvey what one key action I should implement that could further my professional career. Without hesitation he stressed, "Always keep in touch with your associates, clients, suppliers, mentors, coaches and other influential networking groups."

He added, "Make sure you never forget those people who helped you reach the success you have achieved." Always continue to stay connected with your network. Pick up your phone and make the old-fashioned personal phone call. Hearing your voice humanizes your connection, even when you have to leave a voicemail message."

Harvey has always believed that "High-touch one-on-one solidifies much closer connections than emails and high-tech contacts." To make a point, he pulled out his huge contact list. He reached out with a call at least each week to ensure he never lost touch with those who were important to his own personal success. I took to heart Harvey's advice. This was my "wake up call." Now I make personal calls to my industry colleagues at least every week or two, whether on a business or personal basis.

As a recent example, I spoke with Fred, a former colleague who is now semi-retired and moved to Boise, Idaho. I didn't realize his family moved out of California. Fred mentioned he was thinking of writing a book to share his wisdom and successful methods he has implemented during his impressive selling career. I congratulated him and let him know I would help him if he wanted to learn more about becoming an author!

To your health! Keep fit for your healthy mind and body.

Whatever your age, taking care of ourselves has proven to help extend our lives and sharpen our minds. One of my close acquaintances continues to live a vibrant life in spite of several physical setbacks. These challenges include broken ankles, cracked collarbones, severe concussion, chronic altitude sickness, knee problems, foot issues, and the shooting pains of arthritis. These incidents unfortunately disrupted opportunities he was no longer able to experience in his burgeoning athletic career.

Rather than give up and feel sorry about his inability to perform on the football field and tennis court, he discovered his new passion for yoga and meditation. A new productive world opened his eyes with excitement and brought an engaging new purpose to his life. So many of us know firsthand what it is like to deal with various health challenges. Life is a beautiful, robust and incredible, yet at times fragile journey. Our wake-up call is to take control of what we can and live healthy, vibrant lifestyle we can celebrate.

Life balance is the food of our souls.

In our quest for success, we all need to recharge our batteries. Try not to let frustration take control of you. If you aren't doing it now, seek ways to relax outside of your daily work. Finishing your job every day exhausted with nothing to look forward to is not healthy for you or your home life. Sometimes we find the answers right in front of us.

Years ago, my 5 year-old daughter Cyndi asked if she could go to work with me when making my rounds of local sales visits. Considering her surprising request, I announced, "Okay, get yourself all dressed up and let's go to work together!" Not only did we both have lots of fun, but my daughter discovered what I did during my work day. This outing also provided multiple perks. I wrote up more business due to Cyndi's infectious smile, blonde curls, and dimples. Ice cream sundaes were in order to top off that day!

Eleven healthy tips for a more productive lifestyle

• Manage your schedule. Don't let it manage you.

• Take care of your worst items first." It's amazing how much better and more energetic you will feel for the rest of your workday.

• Every week, engage yourself in something you really enjoy, would like to explore. Perhaps participate in an activity you may like but have never done before.

• There are a multitude of activities for us: yoga, reading books, playing cards, taking day trips, joining your child at Boy Scout or Girl Scout Camp, learning to cook, taking horseback riding lessons, motorcycle riding, skydiving, fly fishing, or perhaps joining the legendary Franchise All-Star Band. Your possibilities are endless!

• Make sure your vacations are truly vacations

• Set up your voicemail and autoresponder messages before you leave on a trip.

• Bury your smartphone in the sand. Stop running to Starbucks for their Wi-Fi. Most importantly, when someone asks what you do for a living, don't jump into work mode. Tell them you're a clerk at the local movie theatre. Just smile and your listeners will get the message!

• Don't always be available unless there's a fire you must attend to.

• Limit those emergency work calls to the early morning and keep them short and to the point. With a courteous and friendly voice, remind them you are on vacation, which avoids unnecessary chit-chat.

• Cherish your downtime and start enjoying a glass of wine or iced tea with family and friends. No guilt trips allowed! You deserve the experience.

• Take time to give back to your communities, charities and those in need who are not in a position to help themselves. It's a welcome gesture to help others that are often less fortunate than we are.

See it, believe it. Now it's your time to achieve it!

Make the commitment to celebrate your own world. Today can be your invitation to step out and take your personal journey where you want to grow. It's never a simple mission, but the rewards can be awesome! We all must stay our course and believe in the power within ourselves. Taking our own journeys where we'd like to be certainly is not a "easy walk" It's about our preparation, and personal dedication to achieve our goals.

This is how we will celebrate our own successes whatever they may be it doesn't matter whether you are a homemaker, factory worker, Little League coach, elementary school teacher, painter, candy store owner, inventor, drill sergeant, rocket scientist, ditch digger, orchestra composer or professional ski instructor. If you haven't yet maybe it's time for you to seize your moment We are all empowered to make a difference for ourselves and those around us. Embrace your healthy, wealthy and vibrant lifestyle! It can all be yours if you ignite the power within you.

About the Author

Steve Olson

Steve Olson, CFE and best-selling business author has served as Chief Executive with several corporate and franchising organizations.
Contact: www.olsonandassociates.com

The Wim Hof Method

Wim Hof

Wim Hoff is a Dutch thrill seeker who is recognized worldwide as "Ice Man," due to his incredible ability to withstand extreme cold. Throughout his 58 years, he has achieved amazing feats of daring not thought possible from a human being. Wim Hof has over 23 world records, including one for taking the longest ice bath in history and for completing a full marathon at temperatures close to $-20°$ Celsius.

Wim Hof has repeatedly proven that the impossible was indeed possible. His apparent superpowers have baffled scientists from around the globe: How is he is able to adjust to such extraordinarily cold conditions? The moment Wim Hof submerges himself in ice, all laws of physiology are defied. Hof turns up his "mental thermostat," enabling him to regulate his heartrate, breathing, and blood circulation. Coincidentally, these three body functions are all part of the autonomic nervous system, and Ice Man has spent over 35 years in research and practice to master his control of these functions. He also shares his knowledge with others, teaching people from all walks of life how to do the same.

In 2011, international scientists conducted a formal

investigation on Wim Hof's physiology. The results were stunning. Scientists concluded that human beings are capable of voluntarily influencing both the autonomic nervous system, and immune responses. Prior to this, scientific textbooks declared this to be impossible; but Wim Hof proved otherwise. Ice Man is veritably living proof of what the human body can do. You, too can achieve similar results!

Wim Hof's achievements read like an episode of Superman. Among his more dynamic feats include climbing Mount Everest and Mount Kilimanjaro in only shorts and shoes, taking ice baths for hours at a time, and running a full marathon in the desert heat of 50 o Celsius/122 o Fahrenheit – all without water or food. Hof completed these acts with ease using the "Wim Hof Method," a technique that empowers you to control multiple systems in the body. The most striking effect of this method is one's ability to consciously control the immune system to fight off diseases.

Incredibly, our immune systems influence the prevalence and effects of diseases plaguing the modern world; therefore, current medical thought is focused on ways we can stimulate it to fight back. Wearing clothes and artificially controlling air temperatures at home and work both reduce the natural stimulation of our immune systems. If these physiological layers are muted by environmental modifications, our bodies are no longer in touch with its inner power. This inner power can be awakened in turn by rousing these physiological processes.

The Wim Hof Method addresses this need to stimulate the immune system using the following core practices:

- Breathing & Meditation Techniques
- Cold Shower Therapy
- Full-on Focus (Commitment)

In addition to the benefits to the immune system, these techniques will positively influence mental and physical well-being, along with increased self-awareness and reduced stress levels. Through various workshops, online courses, and expeditions to the Spanish Islands and Africa, thousands have participated in The Wim Hof Method using ice bag immersion.

Join us; take the plunge and reclaim your inner fire.

Testimonials

Countless individuals who practice the Wim Hof Method have described how its breathing techniques and cold therapy have helped them. Here are two examples.

Dutch actress, singer and TV personality Katja Schuurman hosts a reality TV show called *Katja's Bodyscan*. Each episode explores the effects of stimuli on the body, such as sleep deprivation, and in relation to Ice Man, the Wim Hof Method. With the help of Wim Hof, Katja immersed herself in an ice bath, testing her pain limits. The results were incredible, as Katja later shared:

"...Our minds are so capable of controlling the body... I have now been taking cold showers and doing the breathing for over one year. I feel the best-ever..."

Author and entrepreneur Steven E. Schmitt:

"According to Wim Hof, 'The cold is merciless but righteous.'" We can control it by experiencing the power of breathing and unleashing your inner power..."

Three Powerful Pillars

The Wim Hof Method is based on three powerful pillars:

1. Cold Therapy

According to Wim Hof, the cold is your "warm friend." Exposing your body to cold in the right way has enormous benefits, including:

- Aiding in build-up of brown adipose tissue
- Fat loss
- Reduces inflammation
- Helps to balance hormone levels
- Better sleep quality

- Improved and increased production of endorphins, the "feel-good" chemical in the brain that elevates mood.

2. Breathing

Of course, we're always breathing, but we're not always aware of how truly important it is to breathe properly. The Wim Hof Method teaches you to unearth heightened oxygen levels leading to a treasure trove of benefits like:

- Increased energy
- Stress reduction
- An augmented immune system

3. Commitment

This third pillar is the foundation of the other two, as it requires both exposure to cold and conscious breathing, which can only be achieved with patience and dedication. If you're equipped with focus and determination, you can master your body and mind.

Conclusion

By combining and using the elements of the three pillars, you will eventually unlock a multitude of healthy body benefits in the form of:

- Increased energy
- Better sleep
- Heightened focus and determination
- Improved sports performance
- Reduced stress levels
- Greater cold tolerance
- Faster recovery
- Enhanced creativity

Begin your exploration of The Wim Hof Method through:

- Workshops
- Expeditions and
- E-learning

If you're looking for a practical way to become happier, healthier and more powerful, the Wim Hof Method is the right choice for you. Like many gifted people throughout history, Wim Hof was viewed as a crazy man. However, he knew, deep-down that he would change the way people think. He continues to pursue his truth and encourages you to follow your heart, knowing that anything is possible in this world.

About the Author

Wim Hof

Wim Hof is a Dutch extreme athlete known as "The Iceman" for his ability to withstand extreme cold, which he attributes to his Wim Hof Method breathing techniques based on Tibetan Tummo meditation but without its religious components. www.wimhofmethod.com

The Rock
(Journey to Freedom)

Avril Oenone

It was around 1995 and I still vividly remember the day my ex-husband stood over me with a very large rock held high above his head. It was the ultimate situation where my life of low Self esteem had culminated.... I was frozen to the spot. I couldn't move.... Yet deep within I was calm. I was in a bubble. A timeless space of stillness. There were no thoughts... Nothing. I was ready. CRACK!! The rock shattered the white marble hearth to my left! I still sat there motionless with my head bowed. Slowly—very slowly—I raised my head and looked around. It was a very different woman who raised her head...very different as it was from this point I grew. I never did find out what changed his mind but whatever it was I AM grateful for it. That moment changed my life....

Let me take you back to the beginning....

In 1954 I was a girl and the first born to professional parents in a classic 1950's marriage. He controlled the house. She kept it in no uncertain terms. My mother was allocated a fixed sum and managed only that.

Like most women of the time she had absolutely NO idea of my father's income and the house was in his name alone. My mother had NO power. He monitored EVERYTHING. If she needed anything "extra" she had to ask for his approval and prior to any request it was always a good idea to "be nice" to him....

Even at a young age I instinctively recognized this did not sit well with me. Verbally he was a very abusive father and husband. His clever choice of even just a few select words would shred you to ribbons in seconds. Truthfully he NEVER, to my recollection, EVER had a kind word to say about anything or anyone no matter how clever, how beautiful, how hard they worked, or how big their achievement ,or the obstacles they had surmounted.

I worked very hard at school to try to win his approval yet despite my coming consistently top in my class every year he never once congratulated me nor came to see me receive my class prize. Intermittently I would rebel when and how I dared. My five siblings would observe and rarely said a word, let alone supported me. They weren't prepared to shoulder the punishments that followed rebellion. In fact my father controlled us by divide-and-rule tactics.

I was on my own. I desperately needed to be ME yet I was forced to hide behind a facade to survive. I needed genuine support and friendship. It was not forthcoming. So I hid it all deep down inside, put on my armor and fought back. I observed the unjustness of life. I yearned to be a princess in my father's eyes as indeed it seemed my peers were.

I tried the only way I knew how, which was to prove to be worthy of value and my standards were high. To be loved unconditionally for being ME.

I worked incredibly hard—ironically for HIM not ME! I denied myself the love I yearned for and so desperately needed. I didn't love myself and I didn't feel loved.

The times I had any boyfriends that were kind and treated me well I very quickly ended the relationship. I just couldn't handle it. The "bad" boys were the ones I wanted. The ones who would treat me the way I was used to being treated—badly! It was all I knew. What I had was low self esteem and I was in a perpetual cycle of self sabotage. Back then things about which I knew nothing let alone understood.

I was however an intelligent, talented and perceptive child and would do exceedingly well at whatever I put my energies into IF I was interested.... I was interested in esoteric things, mysteries, the Pyramids, the Bermuda Triangle. I grew crystals in my mother's fridge and made up the 3D sacred geometric shapes from their nets. I loved mathematics in particular geometry and creating things by hand. I also loved making my own clothes and subsequently became very interested in fashion after all it was the 1960's. A wonderful time in which to be alive. I loved it all and hid my troubles.

Everyone thought I was confident. No one knew the real me. Unprepared, I left home at 17 with my then boyfriend whom I later married on finding myself pregnant incurring yet more verbal abuse from my father and disapproval from my mother. I later miscarried.

I was unfairly fired from my first full time job whilst being blamed for a huge mistake made by my employer. Yet more parental disapproval and lower still self worth.

Through working all the hours available I made it to a prestigious art school in London to study Fashion and Textiles. My dream course at the best college, which was no mean feat. I didn't settle for second best in that way but I did sell myself short in other ways.

However, I fell pregnant halfway through the course—more sabotage—and had to take a year out after which things were never quite the same. Life took a completely different turn. Within months I was pregnant again. This time with twins. Instead of congratulations from family all I got was, "Oh no! Not again!"

Around this time I had been diagnosed with gall stones and I wasn't satisfied that having my gall bladder removed was the answer. Instinct told me to seek other solutions. So it was at this point I began my search for alternative ways to resolve issues which most people would have accepted lying down.

I was resolute and determined. Giving up was NOT an option in my book. No! That to me WAS failure and I wasn't having anymore of that!

I was fortunate to find Michael Van Straten a local naturopathic doctor who advised me to adopt a vegetarian/vegan diet. This was VERY radical back then. My sheer determination to overcome paid off. I transitioned and now forty years later no more gall stones and gall bladder still intact.

Despite my being pregnant with baby number four we decided to move lock, stock, and barrel to Scotland with the idea of self sufficiency and back to the land ideology.

Great if your partner is of hardworking ilk. Mine, however, was not and the heaviest burdens fell on me.

I STILL hadn't identified my underlying issue and here I was running away hoping to start a new life not having resolved anything but taking it all with me to face even bigger challenges. It doesn't work like that though.... You actually have to SEE and ACCEPT before you can begin to change. It's ALL about taking personal responsibility in EVERYTHING.

Soon I was expecting my sixth child and at three months gestation I found out my husband was having an affair. He subsequently deserted me saying that HE could no longer cope! I was devastated and my self esteem was lower than it had ever been.

It was now 1986. The next five years were a battle for survival and to keep my head above water. Every moment of every day was full including deep into many nights when I would be altering clothes to earn barely enough to do just that.

A 'brief' affair gave me my last child and almost broke me along with everything else. Looking after myself was minimal as the children came first and doing any soul searching to discover myself was a distant dream.

Then in 1991 I met my second husband who appeared to be genuinely interested in me and my large family. I could barely believe it having had all previous dates run off into the sunset never to be seen again the moment they knew I had seven children. To be honest at the time I didn't really blame them.

He convinced me he was genuine and moved in. We married soon after. Almost overnight he changed. The drinking started and the pretense could no longer be kept up. He had by then as most abusers do isolated me from my mother and my friends and the routine abuse started. I had always lived rurally and this house was no different. My nearest neighbors about half a kilometre away seemed oblivious to my situation.

After five years of abuse came that fateful day with the rock. The day something deep inside me shifted.... The ME inside had FINALLY had ENOUGH. I was FREE from his control and FREE to BE ME!!!!!!!

The next few years weren't without their challenges but I grew stronger every day moment by moment.

It took me the next seven years of struggle, self analysis and various experiences to grow sufficiently to finally turn my life around. It was then in 2001 that I became aware of internet dating and signed up. I was going to FINALLY BE ME no matter what...!

My personal profile contained these very words....

I have seven children.

I don't like cooking.

I don't like cleaning.

There. I DID it!!

It was hardly surprising I didn't get any serious contenders except for one and even then it was nine months before I was ready to meet him in person. The man who I have now been with for the last 16 years and who is also my husband.

Finally I was in the driving seat and I LOVED it.

The last 16 years I have been genuinely supported in every way and have had the freedom to pursue my self development to where I am now. I AM in control of my own power and am here to help YOU find Yours.

I have spent time developing my personal creative talents from years ago to be able to create a thriving designer millinery business over that time.

I have given talks and demonstrations to local groups large and small with much success giving me the confidence as a speaker and to promote my business at the same time.

I have given talks and demonstrations to local groups large and small with much success giving me the confidence as a speaker and to promote my business at the same time.

I also give much Love and Gratitude to my husband Dave Richer for heroically coping with all my ventures and unilateral decisions during these years.

I combine my life's experiences along with ALL my training to help my clients become healthy in Mind, Body, and Soul be it locally or globally.

About the Author

Avril Oenone

I AM Avril Oenone Soul Healer.
I look forward to being of service to you
website: www.avriloenonespirithealer.com
Facebook: avriloenonespirithealer/
Email: avriloenone@hotmail.com

Back to Nature

Nhu Nguyen

The lack of knowledge of self-care awareness caused many burdens in my family. I could never forget my grandpa looked; he was exhausted from pronounced coughing, phlegm, having trouble breathing, and grumpy all the time. It was heart wrenching, but his children wouldn't dare reach out to him due to the sickness cause him to be very temperamental. The day I left for the U.S., he put his hand on my shoulder, and said: "Try to find some medicine for me over there, will you?" The promise weighed on my shoulder, but dear grandpa, I was so busy making ends meet in a strange country with strange people. Ten months after I left Vietnam, my grandpa passed away and I still haven't found a single pill to send home. That feeling of guilt had not faded away, then a few years later my uncle passed away from severe tuberculosis, leaving his wife and a little child behind. What a life! Where to find great medicine, where to find them free? Stories like my family are still happening everywhere, causing pain and suffering for countless others....

There were many questions that keep burning in me; what to do to help people escape the pain of illness, live without depression, and believe in the capability healing of our bodies by practicing a natural exercise instead of taking pills? What exercise is good for everyone that no discriminating religions, classes, or genders?

Back to Nature Body and Mind Qigong is a wonderful answer I found. Back to Nature does not only help me recover my health from an almost broke down person become a helpful one, it also helps many practitioners improve their health significantly.

Back to Nature is a practical method that enables practitioners to return to nature and utilize human energy with nature's energy to recover and improve health, both physically and mentally.

The nature, sky, and earth are giant energy sources that coordinate nicely to nurture all living beings in the world. Back to Nature names this giant energy source Nature Taoism. Lava flows inside of the earth and generates the energy of the planet's magnetic field at the South and North Poles. Our planetary orbit is the result of a perfect balance of energy between the earth and sun. On our planet's crust, the water cycle variation and other living things in nature is the energy cycle that nurtures human beings. Back to Nature names this The Living Beings Cycle, or the Tao of Living Beings.

Humans, quite simply, are electrical beings. The nutrition process and survivability of our species is the electrolyte cycle. Our bodies are made up of many different tiny cells; each cell has a positive charge at the cell membrane and negative charge within the substance. Once the negative and positive electricity are imbalanced within a cell, its life will malfunction and gradual destruction will start, causing sickness.

According to the concept of Back to Nature, all materials in nature have a negative volume charge related to its weight and essence. Because we are an element of nature, the human body also has a negative charge. Thanks to this, it helps us balance positive charges generated by life activities: the nutrition process, the breathing cycle, muscle use, brain activity, communication, exposure to artificial light or sunlight, and more. However, due to the high amount of positive charge generated, the negative charge cannot generate the same. This causes a positive and negative charge imbalance in our body.

Practicing Back to Nature qigong aims to increase and balance electrolyte charge within our cells. Once the negative and positive electricity are balanced, the renewable energy cycle within our body occurs automatically. Through time and with proper nutrition, our health will recover when the endocrine system functions are restored. However, to balance our body, where can we obtain the negative charge? This is the main point of the Back to Nature qigong, the main element of why we should return to nature. Nature is not only the natural sights or places that provide us food and habitation. It is also the fundamental energy for us to practice in order to have a healthy body and peaceful mind.

Nature is full of electrical energy sources that balance our body's electrolyte system. There are colorful things in nature and each color has its own special energy. Heat and brightness from sunshine is the necessary energy for almost all plants and humans to develop. Water is the basis of energy for all living beings. The natural world is awash in the sounds of waterfalls, waves, wind, and rain; each having its own energy. The ground has a huge amount of negative electricity if we know how to utilize it correctly. Even plants carry beautiful energy due to the circulation of sap within trees.

Staying with endless natural energy, what a blessing it is to be human! It is even more of a gift for us to return to nature, harmonizing with it and utilizing natural energy to balance ourselves, thereby helping nature to increase its abundant beauty. With that meaning, Back to Nature maximizes the natural energy concept in practice. Applying heat and cold energy in nature helps practitioners to improve internal chi. Implementing water in practice minimizes the risk of injury during special training. Utilizing processes in nature such as thunder, lightning, wind, and clouds creates wonderful breathing techniques and beneficial movement. Back to Nature also applies the vegetation energy in training to help practitioners connect their chi with that found in plants. Walking barefoot on the ground or grass is the basic requirement to connect the ground's negative electric system with our cells to balance the disorder chi in the body. This negative charge improves our nervous system, balances meridians, and recovers internal chi within our organs.

Nature is a warm and loving place for humans to grow stronger, both mentally and physically. Mother Nature can help us rebalance things that through time, due to our mistakes, we have lost the balance of our body and mind. According to Back to Nature, the existence of tangible or intangible materials in the world is referred to as vibration energy. This is considered to be the breath of nature. It is one of the reasons why Back to Nature practitioners have to pronounce when practicing breathing with either Back to Nature body or mind qigong. The roar of thunder and lightning is the breathing method entailed in this concept. Thunder and lightning is the roar of the sky and has an awful power. Each person has their own roar.

There are three roar types in everyone: the roar of communication, the roar of emotions from our heart, and the roar of willingness from our brain. Roar breathing is the method of combining these three types of roars united with our breath, utilizing the potential recovery and development of the human body. Moreover, the vibration of roar breathing generates more positive electricity within our cells in a beneficial way. When we are grounded, the negative electricity of our cells will be connected to and charged by the negative electricity of the ground. In turn, our body's electrical capacity will increase; the higher the capacity is increased, the more energy we have.

Thanks to this method, many Back to Nature practitioners escape from respiratory diseases such as asthma, allergies, tuberculosis, and shortness of breath. Psychological conditions such as depression, fear, and anxiety make way for happiness and optimistic laughter. High blood pressure, high cholesterol, and diabetes resolve. Gout, while usually a stubborn ailment, is also easily cured. Dizziness, headache, and fading memory that occurs mainly in the elderly are reduced, thanks to the Back to Nature breathing technique. Other illnesses such as the common cold, flu, constipation, and urine leakage no longer present a problem, according to many students. Serious sickness such as cancer, on the other hand, is viewed more positively. Along with these special training techniques of Back to Nature, it helps enormously when combined with traditional medical treatment.

If being grounded is the first technique that helps us balance bioelectricity to recover our health, roar breathing is the second technique that harmonizes the breath of practitioners with nature's breath. Harmonizing our breath with nature is a beautiful experience of love and opens the door to enlightenment in evolving physically and spiritually. Love is the harmonic energy interaction between humans and living beings in nature, helping us to evolve better. We are the most evolved of all creatures in the world. The difference between humans and other creatures is the nonstop evolution of our physical body and mind due to a burning desire; other creatures evolve due to adaptation to their outer environment.

Love is the essence point for the connection of human energy and nature. According to Back to Nature, the flow of negative electricity between humans and nature can also occur without direct material contact. This cycle occurs when there is an unconditional kindness within our heart and having an open soul, without the conscious ego dictating reality. When this happens, our negative electricity flows with the outer environment. This is the reason why our health recovers and our skin has a healthier glow after a sightseeing picnic. It is the reason why we feel excited to see a loved one or enjoy a beautiful flower. It is the excitement and joy we experience while enjoying the scenery and the optimistic, nature-loving behavior that creates a perfect electronegative balance between the body and environment.

Living behavior is the basic level and the assessment of each person's psychophysiology level. Positive or negative behavior is the key for our energy to be connected with nature and vice-versa. A big, purposeful life with an open heart and compassion helps the world become more beautiful is called love, which is the Back to Nature mind qigong heart. Love plays a vital role in human evolution; better evolution is the mission of every person in the world. Likewise, nature supports this mission. The only way that practitioners can walk with nature and receive the endless nature energy when they conduct themselves in love. It's not only about the movements and breathing techniques, but also love is the element that dedicates a successful practitioner. Love is the best attraction point and natural energy catches so that practitioners can enter the door of Nature Taoism.

Sky—Human—Earth are three fundamental elements in the worldview of my Vietnamese ancestors. Human is the bridge between Sky and Earth. Earth is the basis of the Human material life. Sky is the Human open spirit. Human cannot be whole without the connections of Sky and Earth. To complete the word Human, we must have the support from the Earth and the guidance from the Sky. Without Earth, there would be no basis for material to exist. Without Sky, there would be no purpose and direction for life, and the human spirit will be lost on the path of evolution. Reestablishing the connection between Human to Sky and Earth completes the Human within the three elements are the primary condition, as well as the basis for all development of the body and mind.

I strongly believe, the beauty of nature awakes the beauty in our soul, helps us to be back to our pure, original selves; a loving heart that is full of humanity. Back to Nature is the path to achieve the whole Human, recover health, and evolve our body and spirit. Being Back to Nature means anyone can learn this precious lesson anywhere. We can use this way to overcome our body's hindrances, return to a peaceful mind, and harmonize ourselves with endless natural energy. Back to Nature is the path to achieve health, happiness, and a nonbinding life.

Let's get Back to Nature!

About the Author

Nhu Nguyen

Author/Certified Therapist/Qigong Trainer/Vice President of Hoan Nhien (Back to Nature) Nonprofit Organization.

Back to Nature is an Nonprofit Organization 501 (c) (3). EIN# 46 – 3740615

Together, let's light up the world. Your support will help countless people

For more information, please visit us at:
- www.naturebreathing.com
- Amazon book: "Back to Nature and Breathing"
- Email: nhunguyen@naturebreathing.com

Wish you healthy and mindfulness!
I'm looking forward to hearing from you!

Mind, Body, Consumption, and the Life I Attract

Perris Turner

Every human being's journey starts off as a nice story, at least from conception. However, depending on what environment you're conceived within determines the rabbit hole from which you emerge.

There's a saying: "Grandma can love you so much that the bottom belly goes bust!" Translation: too much love through food can kill you, and I mean literally. Food affects our brain, hormones, and how we feel. If you're not educated, you wouldn't think food could affect the way you think and live, but it does in a major way.

All of my grandparents passed away from the complications of metabolic diseases. Breast cancer and prostate cancer on my mother's side, Type 2 diabetes and dementia on my father's side. Many relatives in my family suffer from metabolic syndrome diseases. One of my cousins died of a stroke in his late 20s. The systemic problem is a lack of awareness. So many people are not privy to the value of the health and wellness lifestyle.

This is especially true when you look at the population that lives below the poverty line. Healthier food choices are either too expensive or not accessible locally. When you mention health and wellness to some people, it sounds like a country club to them. If someone wanted a better quality of food or produce, they would have to travel outside their community to get a better selection of non-GMO options.

Malnutrition in America has reached epidemic levels and is particularly destructive to the black community. This is by design of the environment, demanding a response as it has a deep impact on mental programming. The roots of this go back many generations, post indigenous native land. Processed foods today are killing minority communities and the American population as a whole. I guess you can say the masses can become enslaved if they're not conscious of the importance of living an overall healthy lifestyle.

Food addiction is a serious issue. I've always said the companies that create these sugary foods we crave and love to eat are probably the most notorious drug dealers. The consensus is that we have more overweight and sickly people than any other time in the history of the human race. Never before in U.S. history have we had more metabolically diseased and overweight people. Seventy percent of Americans are considered overweight, according to the standards set by our government, and the information classifies people who are actually overweight as normal weight. My theory is that there are more people in the United States who are fat-mass heavy in weight than statistics actually report.

The majority of overweight people are addicted to food and cannot control their caloric intake. They desire more calories than their bodies need. The reasons they crave unhealthy foods in unhealthy quantities are numerous. When we eat these calories that are concentrated in oils, sugars, and fast foods, they are designed to rush into the bloodstream very rapidly as if you've been injected with a needle. The result is a drug high because these foods signal the dopamine receptors in the brain to spike. Because of this, there's a craving for more of the same foods and you can't stop thinking about recreating the taste and chasing that same high. The brain becomes insensitive to dopamine over time from the caloric rush and the same amount of calories no longer satisfies you, resulting in the need to go after more calories.

People who eat like this do not receive enough micronutrients such as vitamins, minerals, trace minerals, phytochemicals, antioxidants, and fatty acids. It's not likely that the nutrients found in vitamin supplements can fill the gap. There are thousands of nutrients the human body requires from a broad spectrum of food to support normal brain function. Foods that are micronutrient deficient trigger a signal to overconsume calories.

Drug use, food abuse, and food addiction have the same effect. You feel really good when you're doing it, but then when you try to stop it, you feel pain. It's just like cocaine and smoking cigarettes; when you build up these toxic metabolites in your tissues from the processed and fast foods, your body accumulates more free radicals. You have more of what is called advanced glycation end products, or AGE. This can ignite diabetes, destroying the nerves and causing amputations from the buildup within the tissue.

When there's an attempt to lose weight without proper nutrient management, it's a very hard task to accomplish. If you can lose weight, the next obstacle is to sustain the weight loss. The unhealthy body is biologically designed to keep eating food due to the nutrient deficiency, which is equivalent to nutrient starvation. Because the person yearns for comfort food, they eat more than they should. They become uncomfortable when they stop eating, and feel the need to keep their digestive tract busy. They overeat, which leads to being overweight. It's a cycle that never ends. People who are severely overweight and nutrient deficient have a more challenging task of becoming healthier.

At the young age of 28, I was diagnosed with prehypertension. My systolic and diastolic reading measured 150/95. As I stood 5'-7" and weighed over 200 pounds, circumstances didn't tip in my favor. The common symptoms I experienced were daily headaches, nightly acid reflux, terrible anxiety, and adrenal fatigue that robbed me of my youthful energy. Daily aspirin for my headaches and shoulder inflammation, the need to sleep in an upright position, and dark blotches forming on my cheekbones were some of the consequences I suffered. A deeper, more profound consequence of it all was my faulty belief system and all the stories I accepted as truth. I habitually operated from the conditioning that affected my choices and attracted DIS-EASE in my life, mirroring a reflection of sickness. From a matrix perspective, the word *dis-ease* is commonly used by quacks; but through my eyes, it's the antonym of *ease*.

Monitored cleansing and fasting in addition to a change of eating habits and lifestyle definitely put a stop to my inevitable road to disaster. When someone tries to stop eating for a few hours, the body tries to get rid of free radicals. They're weak, shaky, and may experience a headache. Anxiety spikes and their body feels like crap. The brain's response is to keep eating food. People commonly think of these stimuli as detox symptoms, but I think of them as proof of self-repair.

Over the years, I have changed my eating habits and morphed my body. My mind was the first thing I needed to detox. The body is an instrument for my mind to play as it will. It was a journey that took due diligence, commitment, focus, responsibility, honor, trust, and a combination of all other principles I've learned. I paid the price day in and day out to keep the balance. Some days were better than others, but overall I lost the weight in fat mass. My blood pressure today is very healthy, usually reading 107/78. Athleticism and activities throughout my youth and high school years maintained my fitness. I played Pop Warner football, ran track competitively, and was a great amateur gymnast. Being young and having good physicality was my ally. Combine that with minimum stress despite going to school, life was smooth sailing. That was until circumstances started to change.

During my first year of college, the pendulum started to swing in a different direction. I became a teenage father at 18. Maintaining my grades in school and also providing for my son was a huge challenge. With my new environment, I developed serious stomach issues due to the stress. When you pay child support before you're 18 and have extra financial responsibilities with no sustainable income, life can become difficult very quickly. My resolution was to join the United States Navy. That way, I would have some form of steady income and means to continue my education.

When I reflect on my time in the military, it taught me a lot about myself, both mentally and physically. Waking up at 2:00 or 3:00 in the morning and going through the rigorous academic and physical training definitely helped shape my disciplined nature. Being that young from the rough streets of South Los Angeles said one thing though…that I was programmed!

Looking back at my behavior in boot camp was one of the

first signs that my environment had conditioned me. I once had words with the head commanding officer of the flight crew on my aircraft carrier while on deployment out to sea. Receiving EMI (Extra Military Instruction) on a regular basis was not my career path, especially when I had to clean the sump tanks on a nuclear aircraft carrier the size of three football fields. Can you imagine the shower I had to take to get the smell of ocean stench from my pores? I learned fast and adapted to my new environment by realizing how nonverbal or verbal expression sets the tone, builds rapport, and stages the manner of interaction. Gradually, I moved up the ranks to E5 and was honorably discharged. I'm grateful and proud that I served and wouldn't change anything I experienced.

The 42 year-old man that shares his story today is a completely different person from that period of time. You see, I am awake and have definitely taken the red pill, as a reference to the movie, *The Matrix*. I constantly experience newfound paradigm shifts, improving my perspective on deeper mental, physical, and spiritual levels. I have reprogrammed my mind to be comfortable with being uncomfortable. That's the only way I accept and believe in attracting what I want. My higher thinking faculties, consciously when in tune and in harmony with these laws, will create quantum change that jumps ahead.

I am absolutely grateful that I have the awareness, humility, and confidence to share this with you. You see, there was a time when I was a mouse in the rat race, just chasing the cheese. I lived life day-to-day, focusing on whatever my heart was programmed to desire, unaware of definitive value. I was conditioned to the ordinary, trivial, and commonplace things that I thought I wanted.

Belief systems are not only conditioned subconsciously, but also has a effect consciously. Our beliefs are inherited dating all the way back to our ancestors. They were built right into the DNA of our genepool. These are involuntary systems working on autopilot and wired to the autonomic nervous system. Your thoughts are in synch with the endocrine hormonal system, affecting emotions and the vibrations of the body. Simply put, we think, feel, release, and attract. The law of cause and effect deals its card. Learning how to have dominion over my mind, overcoming fear subconsciously; putting it behind me so it can push me forward towards courage is key. I take the initiative to polarize my perspective, swinging the pendulum towards my purpose.

While growing up, I witnessed a lot of sparing between people when situations became heated because of different values and perspectives. Remember, environment always demands a response. If you observe any social group, no matter what race or creed, combining low self-esteem with no clear definitive understanding of value and with little opportunity, the outcome more than likely leads to some form of miscommunication, confusion, abuse, or reactive behavior. No matter what nationality, when people have not been socially experienced to handle things proactively and responsibly when they're upset or angered, not knowing how to express their values, frustration and problems will occur.

Traumatic experiences further compound beliefs that outwardly show in behavior. These layers of estimated experiences equate to a person's value and how they see themselves. The trifecta of these experiences occur in the home environment, outside environment, and carried within the individual. I myself couldn't avoid the in- and outgoing tides of my outside environment, even though I grew up in a loving home. I was robbed at gunpoint as a teenager and had my share of scuffles growing up.

A couple of my childhood friends went to prison and five were murdered from the consequences of living the gang lifestyle. However, I never succumbed to that outside pressure of the gang culture. The love that was in my home provided me with a stable environment and I knew I was loved. There was no urge to participate in the bullshit. As kids, my friends and I would go out and do all the things that boys would do, but there was a certain gut feeling that I knew if something was wrong, I'd listen to that inner voice in my head. That was instilled in me at an early age and I would never do something that I felt wasn't right.

The kids that started hanging with the wrong crowds when they were older did what all normal children do; they played with their hot wheels and tonka toys, watched cartoons, and did all the activities that little boys loved to do. The problem with kids who struggled in rough neighborhoods was the lack of having a stable environment in the home.

Now, I'm not saying that there was no love, good times, and a feeling a self-worth and value growing up in my environment.

Every perspective of lower vibration has a polar opposite that vibrates higher. I am a product of this storyline. I want to bring focus and light on the fact that when you've been influenced by your surroundings, it has a significant impact on how you see yourself, those around you, how we interact with others, and affects the choices we make. My story is about how I broke the padlock of harmful indoctrination and mortifying negative feedback; indoctrination of environment, genetics, ancestors, parents, religion, people—but most importantly—myself. It's about discovery and finding out that I AM the programmer, so I can rewrite my own programs and begin with goals and purpose in mind.

This is about epigenetically trumping genetic deterioration, mentally, and physically, rewriting my script, and leaving an indelible imprint. All human beings are ordinary people that can make extraordinary agreements. But when you look from God's perspective, all humans are extraordinary and can create limitless and infinite agreements.

My *why* is to inspire the inner faith and freedom of mind so that others can create the liberty they desire. My *how* is through character, exhibiting the principles aligned with my values. It consciously polarizes positive thoughts in my mind and influences my goals. I execute my vision for the day and govern my home and outside environment to create liberty. On a daily basis, I use the knowledge and wisdom I have acquired. My *what* is through the service of health wellness coaching and living.

About the Author

Perris Turner

Perris Turner - Health Coach, Speaker, Investor
polarize2vision@gmail.com

Awaken Your Inner Voice—
Reclaim Your Health and
Happiness Using Your Intuition

Keri Fulmore

*"It is essential to remember that only the mind can create,
and that correction belongs at the thought level"*
—*A Course in Miracles.*

I have always believed that health is wealth. In fact, I made it my life purpose. I made conscious decisions about the food I bought, what I put in my mouth, and made sure that I moved my body to stay healthy and fit. Health was my whole life and purpose. I made sure that I ate only organic foods, ate them in their whole form, and kept sugar intake very low. I managed my weight, exercised, slept eight hours, took my vitamins, and treated my body like a sacred temple.

I had studied Traditional Chinese Medicine graduating in 2004, researched nutrition and vitamins extensively, became certified in Functional Medicine, and developed my intuition to help people get to the root of their health imbalances.

But do you know what? I still could not stop what was

coming. Like a ghost train, I did not even see it until it hit me. What if I told you that I had to learn the hard way, that caring for your physical body by looking outward, is not as important as you think?

I am not saying that eating right, and exercising is not important. I'm saying it is not everything. I learned that true health begins on the inside. That, if you want to lead a life of vibrant health, you need to be connected to your mind, body and emotions, your intuition, and most importantly how well you treat yourself. This was something I did not do very well.

My story begins in December 2012. I had just moved across the country with my husband and two kids to be closer to family. I had just opened up an acupuncture clinic and offered medical intuitive readings online to help people heal.

My life was falling into place and for the first time, I felt happy. I was happy with work, my body, and with life. I was happy to be able to help family. I felt so lucky; I was doing everything right.

The Eye of the Storm

That is when I started to notice a pressure in the back of my head. I was not too concerned about it; I knew that a good chiropractic adjustment must be what I needed. I found myself in the chiropractor office the next day. Everything went as expected. I got my adjustment, felt much better, and headed home. The pressure was gone.

When I arrived home, I laid my daughter on the floor to change her and stood up. at was the moment my life changed forever. Like a flash of lightning, I went from being completely normal and good in my body, to every inch of it, from the top of my head to the bottom of my feet, riddled in burning, stinging, and searing nerve pain. Panic filled my entire being. My heart pounded in my chest, my mind raced, my breathing felt shallow, my body feeling like a twisted and wrung out towel, suddenly feeling like I was going to pass out. I found myself on the living room floor on my hands and knees calling for my husband.

I knew I was in trouble. My husband found me on the floor in a panic. Immediately, we landed ourselves in the Emergency Room. I'm really not sure what I would have done without him.

After a battery of tests on me, they told me to stand up, but I felt like I couldn't. It was if someone had attached a rope to my head and was pulling me down to the ground. It felt like the ground was pulling me in. My body ached and burned, my muscles felt twisted, my body shaking on the inside and nothing. I was told that there was nothing wrong with me. They discharged me to go home and call my doctor in the morning. This was the longest night of my life. What could I have possibly done to deserve this? I found myself thinking about what I did to cause this. I was healthy, right? I barely slept that night as the pain was tremendous. I felt like my body was on re from head to toe and the tears would not stop. It felt like my body had been hijacked by terror, or like there was a terrorist attack happening inside my body. This was my story for the next Five years of my life: immense burning pain, tremors, and heartache.

Every doctor I went to said the same thing. They had no idea what was going on. I was scanned, had MRI's, and put through every test imaginable. The battery of tests found nothing. I was completely normal on paper, but I was not even close! The more I was told this, the more hopeless I felt. How could I be on fire constantly and nothing be found wrong? I remember wishing that there was at least some kind of diagnosis because then I could at least begin to heal myself. I'm not sure what was worse: the pain that ripped through my body or the fact that nobody could find anything wrong with me. I was in my own personal hell. I was a prisoner of my body. It was a perfect storm.

I remember when my neurologist told me that he thought it was all in my head from postpartum depression. He told me to take antidepressants and it would all go away. I was not depressed. Remember, I was happier than I had ever been! But, this got me wondering just how much of this was truly in my mind or how much I was not paying attention.

This went on and on. I saw doctors, chiropractors, osteopaths, naturopaths, healers, and psychics, but no one could offer me any help. I spent every day crying, wondering how I could live like this. I remember the day the pain tried to take my hope. I don't know if you have ever experienced widespread body pain before, but it can feel like one continuous torture sentence. My hope and faith that I would heal quickly diminished. I was slipping into depression, feeling like I was being punished for something I had done.

At this point, I knew I had a choice to take matters into my own hands or lose all hope. I decided that it was time to take my power back! I was not going to let this beat me. I knew from countless intuitive sessions that there was always a root cause and that somehow this was my greatest gift. I knew that if I could just put aside my own beliefs and thoughts, I could get to the underlying gift beneath. I knew that in that gift there was a profound healing!

Taking my Power Back!

That is when I decided that no one was going to be able to help me but me. I had two beautiful daughters and a husband that loved me. I had to find a way out of this. I had always been intuitive. I had been helping people for years to find the root cause of their health issues, so why couldn't I do it for myself? What was I waiting for?

No one was going to save me, except me. It was in this moment that I knew I had to look within. I had to put aside my ego and attachment to wellness to be an observer and hear my inner voice. I knew that I could not access my intuition from a place of panic. The first rule of thumb when looking into other people is to make sure you are in a relaxed state. So, I started to meditate.

At this point I had been reading stories of people who had healed themselves, who had medical conditions that they were able to overcome. I read of Anita Moorjani who had Stage 4 lymphoma, whose organs were shutting down, and then had a near death experience. She connected with pure unconditional love in that moment, and knew that if she chose to come back and love herself unconditionally, her cancer would heal and disappear. A few weeks later, her cancer was found to be gone!

Reading this story and stories like it inspired me. I began to meditate on a daily basis. If I could connect to the unconditional love and my inner voice, surely, I could heal too. Meditation is a hard thing to do when your body is in head to toe pain. But somehow, I was able to put aside my attachment to being pain-free and the pain itself. I became an observer, I trained myself to watch my story, my pain flowed past me like a river. I surrendered to the outcome. All I knew was that I was going to find some answers.

One day during my meditation when I felt at peace in my mind, I decided to ask a question: "Body, why am I in pain?" The answer came out of nowhere, a bit like the pain perhaps. I started to wonder if things coming out of nowhere just might be my specialty. But the answer came straight back at me. "Because you don't love yourself!" Now this threw me out to left field and my ego had a good time with this one. *But of course, I love myself,* I thought. Only the more I thought about it, the more I realized I didn't.

I had been hard on myself my entire life. I compared my body to others, I was unkind to her when I looked in the mirror, I felt less than because I was not perfect. It might not have been the answer I was seeking, which was to fix it with natural remedies, but it sure was a truth I had ignored for a long time. My body was expressing the pain I had about myself in a physical way! I had to learn to love myself. You know what got me loving myself more? It was more than just looking in the mirror and saying "I love you" to myself.

My inner voice showed me that all I had to do was love myself like I would love a newborn baby. I told myself that. I was as loveable as a new born baby, perfect just the way I was! I was shown that my miraculous body allows me to be here in this world. To experience kisses and hugs, tastes of food, the feeling of oxygen filling my lungs and the sun on my skin! *I should treasure her,* I thought.

The more I visualized this love I had for myself in my baby-like state, the more I began to shed that negative Nancy in my mind. The more I gave thanks to my body for allowing me to be here, the more I began to see myself as unconditional love. All of the self-love began to pay off, because my body pain began to decrease in severity. I was able to get out of bed!

Could it be that simple? Realizing that the pain was decreased but not gone, I decided to get quiet with myself some more and dig deeper for more answers. I found myself asking my body what else I needed to do to heal the pain. My intuition was on fire now, coming quickly and swiftly. "You can heal your brain." These were the words I heard. I had no idea what that meant at first. I went on to learn that the brain in chronic pain can literally change and rewire itself, from getting stuck in a pain loop. The next thing I knew, I was retraining my brain with Functional Neurology. This therapy literally uses hand and eye exercises to get your brain to regrow new neural networks around old programs.

I learned that this therapy is what healed Canadian hockey player Sidney Crosby of his concussion syndrome and got him back on the ice. Every hair on my body stood up. I knew from deep inside my gut that this was what I needed. I took action! I listened to my intuition and in six weeks, all of my burning body-wide pain was gone!

The point of this story is that no one told me how to heal myself. In fact, lots of people offered me lots of ways not to heal. Every time I sought answers from outside sources, it ended in failure and frustration. Now, I am by no means saying you should not see a doctor. But remember that the answers to true health, healing, and happiness come from within. The answers are not where you expect them to be. They never are. More often than our egos will give us credit for, the real answers come from within.

Since recovering, I have begun using what I learned to help people suffering from their own challenges, helping them to understand the power of their intuition, and how to connect to it. Every day, I see healing happen when we connect to the answers within. It reaffirms just how powerful our minds really are.

Get quiet with yourself. Go within and ask your inner voice. It always knows what to do! I have learned to always check in with myself, to ask myself how I really feel and make sure I take the time to do something about it. I now use my intuition every day, including what foods I should eat, business decisions, therapies for self-care etc. You can use your intuition for absolutely everything. I believe that in order to live a healthy and vibrant life, that listening to your inner voice is essential. In fact, it is critical!

How to Connect to Your Intuition

Step 1. Get yourself into a relaxed and meditative space by closing your eyes. Take a few deep breaths deep into the belly. Feel your mind relaxing with each breath. Feel every muscle in your body relax.

Step 2. Focus your attention on your heart center. The energy of your heart. Notice if it is contracted, or sad, or depressed. If there is any tension, take a deep breath and see this tension, these emotions releasing from your heart, breathing them out with one deep breath.

Step 3. Focus on something that gives you unconditional love and joy. This could be a memory of the moment your child was born, or when you brought your puppy home. Whatever it is, focus on the feeling it brought to you. Once you can feel that high unconditional love and joy vibration, bring that energy into your heart. See your heart and your entire body filling with unconditional love and joy. Take a deep breath.

Step 4. Move your attention to your third eye (right between your eyebrows in the center of your forehead). Feel the energy of the third eye moving outwards and growing. Keep pushing the energy outward until you feel expansive. Now, you are ready to ask a question.

For example: "Creator/God/Spirit, please show me what I can do today to bring more joy into my life?"

You will hear an answer right away. You may also see a picture or get a feeling. Whatever it is, it will come swiftly and immediately. Listen, and be sure to take action. Remember your intuition is like a muscle the more you use it, the more it grows!

About the Author

Keri Fulmore

Medical Intuitive, Functional Medicine Practitioner
www.intuitivehealthsolutions.com
keri@intuitivehealthsolutions.com

Finding Strength in Stillness

Jon Haas

In today's frantic, fast-paced world of high-speed internet access, instant gratification, and constant contact communication, it is extremely rare for anyone to be able to find quiet, and (even rarer) to find stillness. But stillness is exactly what we need to counterbalance the demanding, breakneck pace set by the modern world. The daily struggles and stresses wear us down, sap our strength, and deplete our energy like no other time in history. Only a practice of carving out time for stillness can fully replenish our deep well of strength. Stillness is a refuge from the chaos of everyday living. It allows us to re-center, refocus, and recharge.

Over the centuries, contemplative monks, long-lived yogis, and powerful martial artists have practiced stillness. Different methods can yield the same results by developing human energetic potential to its highest level. There are many ways of cultivating stillness, but in my experience, the most powerful and profound is the practice of standing meditation.

Zhan Zhuang (Standing Meditation)

Zhan zhuang, or standing meditation exercise, has been used as a method of relaxation and health cultivation for thousands of years. The earliest known reference to standing appears in *The Yellow Emperor's Classic of Chinese Medicine*. Martial arts master Wang Xiangzhai wrote the following in his book on *zhan zhuang*:

> *It is said that already 2000 years ago there existed the book Internal Canon, the gem of Chinese medicine, which even today is a guide for medical practice. The chapter Simple questions concentrates on cultivating health. For example, we can read there: "In ancient times great masters stood on earth, supporting heaven, controlling yin and yang, breathing with essence of qi, standing alone, guarding spirit, with body being as one." Before the eastern Han dynasty many scholars and warriors knew the methods of "tranquil cultivating." The exercises could be done walking, standing, sitting, lying. It was popular form of cultivating health. Later, during reign of Liang dynasty's emperor Wu, Damo came to China to teach. He transmitted methods of "washing marrow" and "changing tendons."*

The health preserving and sustaining effects of *zhan zhuang* have been documented in hospitals and medical clinics across China. The reason this practice has such a profound impact on health and recovery from exercise is that the standing meditation acts like a system-wide reboot for the whole body. It stimulates the nervous system, increases circulation, and raises energy levels, while providing deep relaxation for both mind and body.

Aches, pains, old injuries, muscular tensions, and imbalances are highlighted and brought to the forefront by this method and then slowly dissolved over time and completely released. The practice provides a way of completely relaxing and letting go of the muscular tensions in the body, while the correct alignment of the bones delivers support, creating a profound neutral and relaxed, almost buoyant state. As the whole body and mind are exercised, both relax and stimulate the nervous system, increasing circulation, opening the joints, and raising energy levels for a feeling of overall well-being.

This exercise looks easy from the outside. After all, you're just standing there and not moving. However, there is a lot going on inside: the breath and *qi* (energy) are moving. This exercise is a challenging, sometimes frustrating, yet highly beneficial and rewarding practice. The only way to truly appreciate it is to experience it for yourself.

How Do We Set Up for Standing Meditation?

In practical terms, how should we stand? Let's start with the head and work our way down.

- Begin by standing in a natural stance: feet shoulder width apart and knees slightly bent.
- Lift upward slightly with the crown of the head, as if being pulled up by a string, allowing the chin to lower. This straightens the vertebrae at the back of the neck.
- Shoulders are back and down, sitting on the spine.
- The back should be flat. Do not tuck the pelvis. The spine should be suspended from above like a skeleton hanging in a science classroom.
- Hold your arms in front of your body, level with the solar plexus, as if hugging a tree. There should be a golf ball-sized space under the armpits.
- The bottom of the spine pulls straight down from the tailbone, as if there is a weight attached to the sacrum. You should feel like you are sitting on a high stool yet trying to stand up at the same time.
- Allow the knees to bend slightly. Feet should be shoulder-width apart and pointed forward, as if on railroad tracks.
- Legs should feel like they are squeezing a beach ball. Remember though, the ball puts outward pressure on the legs as they squeeze in, so there is pressure both directions, not just one.
- The weight is carried in the hollow behind the balls of the feet. In Chinese medicine, this is known as the *yongquan*, or bubbling well point.

All of the above points must be maintained to have a truly "natural" standing posture. *Maintaining a relaxed posture is key to beginning your standing meditation.*

How to Supercharge Your Standing Practice

Now that you have the external mechanics down, let's talk about how to supercharge your relaxation process.

1. Mentally scan the body for areas of tension. The usual suspects will be the neck, shoulders, low back, and quads.

2. Begin to actively release each area of tension one by one with your mind. For example, think of the tightness in your shoulders and relax it by telling yourself, "The tightness in my shoulders is letting go and relaxing." Then proceed to the next area until you have systematically gone through them all.

3. If one particular area gives you trouble, then work on breathing into it. Inhale into the area, hold for a few seconds, and then exhale from the area to release it. Repeat this process until all the tension resolves.

4. Once you have removed all the residual tension in the body, continue to stand, holding that relaxed feeling. Think of your body as a drop of ink dissolving in the ocean, spreading out in all directions.

5. Start with 10 minutes of *zhan zhuang* standing. Work up to 30 minutes. In Chinese medicine, it is said that it takes approximately 28 minutes for the blood to complete one full cycle though the body, thus the recommendation to stand for 30 minutes. This can be increased to 60 minutes over time to allow for two full cycles of blood to be completed.

A New (Old) Method of Energy Development and Recovery

The art and science of becoming a stronger, more vibrant, and energetic human being can be broken down into two main methods:

1. The addition of driving forces (yang), and
2. The subtraction of restrictive forces (yin)

When most people train for strength, they focus solely on the *yang of strength*—the addition of driving forces. But this will only get you so far. It's like driving a car around all day with the emergency brake on. You can still get where you need to go, but that extra, unnecessary drag kills the car's performance and guzzles gas (consuming energy).

Where is the hidden drag on your energy?

Residual muscle tension, or tonus, is the continuous, passive partial contraction of muscles in the body that aids in posture and support. Any type of strength training exercise, stress, fear, or trauma will all cause an unwanted and unnecessary increase in the normal residual muscle tension of the body. Usually this extra tonus goes unnoticed, or worse, is simply deemed an acceptable and natural side effect of living. The problem with this added tension is that the continuous contraction of muscle throughout the day, every day, uses up energy. This energy that can (and should) be available to us is being siphoned off, thereby putting the brakes on our performance.

Rather than increasing our energy, freeing our movement, and allowing us to access our full strength potential as human beings, the consistent focus on the *yang of strength* makes us literally muscle-bound.

The Yin of Strength—Standing in Stillness

The *yin of strength*, standing meditation practice, is how we strategically and systematically remove those restrictive forces to reveal our true strength potential as an integrated human being.

In teaching this method to both my fitness clients and martial arts students, I find that in addition to our usual compliment of recovery drills (consisting of mobility exercises, yoga asana, and compensatory movement), the addition of this simple practice of standing meditation has consistently accelerated our recovery process, allowed us to reach new levels of relaxation, and strengthened the mind-body connection beyond any other work we have done. Additionally, it has managed to increase energy levels while fortifying our bodies against the daily rigors of life, work, and family stresses.

While this method is elegantly simple to practice, requires little space and no special equipment, and can be done at virtually any time of day, it also is startlingly deep. Make the time to find stillness in your busy day and you will be surprised to discover new wells of strength, energy, and health, greater than you ever thought possible.

About the Author

Jon Haas

Jon Haas, "The Warrior Coach" has been training in Bujinkan Budo Taijutsu for more than 25 years and is currently ranked as a Kudan (9th degree black belt) under Jack Hoban Shihan. He has also trained in Okinawan Karate, Tae Kwon Do, Russian Systema, BJJ, Krav Maga, as well as Internal Martial Arts of Yiquan and Aiki.He is a certified Underground Strength Coach-Level 2, a certified Personal Trainer as well as founder of Warrior Fitness Training Systems. In 2008, Jon wrote the book, *Warrior Fitness: Conditioning for Martial Arts*, and since then has created numerous other online training and coaching programs helping people around the world become the strongest, most capable versions of themselves!

Contact Information:

Website: www.warriorfitness.org/
Facebook Page: www.facebook.com/WarriorFitnessGym/
YouTube Channel: www.youtube.com/user/WarriorFitness1

Wake Up to Vibrant Health

Kristy Ware

I paced alongside the rectangular table where my friends sat in celebration. I couldn't sit and join them because agonizing pain radiated along the left side of my lower back. The intermittent burning of sciatica made sitting, sleeping, and moving utterly unbearable. I excused myself several times during that dinner (and many other social gatherings) to stretch, adjust, and manage my severe discomfort.

Simple things like hanging out with friends, going for walks, or eating a meal involved too much pain to truly enjoy. I yearned for my body and my life back. I wanted to run, to train again, to throw a softball and be active in the way I loved. I would wake up in the night gripped with not only searing pain, but fear. I was terrified that I might never recover and that my life as I knew it was forever changed.

It is so easy to be consumed with fear in the face of daily excruciating pain. Fearing this was my new reality took me to some very dark and depressing places. What would my life look like if I couldn't be physically active?

From a very young age, I turned to exercise as a coping mechanism when life was uncertain, challenging, or otherwise stressful. I am not talking about a low-key stroll but exercise that demanded more of my body like running, lifting, and pushing every physical limit until I felt satisfied.

During the summer of 2011, I had been biking to and from my summer job between the first and second year of my kinesiology program, while also weight training and playing softball. I enjoyed my life to the fullest. One morning, I awakened feeling strong and fit, but went to sleep that night in debilitating pain that I had never experienced. It crept up mildly like a headache that goes from bearable to all-encompassing and eventually paralyzing. Getting out of bed, getting dressed, and making breakfast proved to be an excruciating task that did not get any easier as the weeks passed. That summer was the first time in over 11 years that I turned to pharmaceutical medication to endure each day. Aleve and Robaxacet became my drugs of choice. I had no idea what was going on with my back or my body, nor did I know how I was going to fix it.

My younger sister was getting married that summer and I was a bridesmaid in her wedding. Not only did that mean a 5-hour flight (with a lot of sitting!) but it also meant I was agreeing to step out of my comfort zone of jean shorts and running shoes to wear a floor-length red satin dress and high heels. It wasn't the ideal set of circumstances for someone with a back injury.

A few weeks before leaving for that trip is when my life as I knew it changed in an instant. I was petrified. I had lost my sense of self, my motivation, and my sex drive. To be totally frank, I came pretty damn close to losing my faith. I am not talking about religious faith here, but the faith that I would not fully heal and recover. I felt for the first time in my life that my body had failed me and I had lost control. I was a Fitness Trainer, I lived for exercise, health, and motivating others to live strong and vibrant lives. Who would I be if I couldn't move?!

After surviving the trip, the long dress, and feeling brain fog every day from the pain meds, I began the second year of my kinesiology program. Many of my classes were physically demanding. As usual, I put a lot of effort, energy, and pressure on myself to succeed—especially since I was a mature student. I felt I had something to prove and could do what the 20-somethings could do! That is until, well, I couldn't. Interesting how life works isn't it?

To really put all of this into context, I was 'that' kid who never sat still, couldn't wait for recess, and played on every sports team all through elementary and high school. Pursuing a career in the fitness industry was an obvious choice. What was most interesting to me at that time was that even when things seem aligned and I believed I was on my path, the universe still put challenges in my way.

I want to take a moment now and rewind 25 years. From the time I was a child, my point of reference for how one proceeds when faced with trauma, illness, or injury was medically based and full of worry and fear. This does not come as a surprise given that my brother was born with severe spina bifida, hydrocephalus, and only expected to live three days. Not only was his mere survival in question but also his quality of life and mental capacity. Medical intervention was what I knew and how I learned to cope.

The memory that is most imprinted on my mind from the age of 8 was when I walked into the hospital for the first time to both meet and potentially say goodbye to my little brother. It was scary, to put it lightly. Tubes were coming out of his body at every angle. His fragile torso lay still, clinging to life. His oversized head was positioned with rollers to one side. I stood, shocked. The first words I spoke to him were, "Hi, Richard. I'm your big sister, Kristy."

Growing up with a sibling that was given a mere three days to live is not an easy hand to be dealt. But he defied all odds and survived four major surgeries in his first three years of life. The whole family stood by his side, instilling courage and hope into this little soul I call my brother, and we call a miracle.

Most of my childhood involved a lot of hospital visits. Although the trips became less frequent and we were finally able to bring him home when he was 4, my brother's conditions became more complex and always near death. As an adolescent, I recall our home as a revolving door of nurses, therapists, relief workers, disimpaction regimens; a stream of unfamiliar faces providing care to my very delicate sibling. Life was a constant worry of death, fear of the unknown, and whether the medical teams in place could keep my brother going and if my family could brave the physical and emotional challenges that accompanied his survival.

Not surprisingly, at age 21 I began taking anti-depressants and anti-anxiety drugs, among many others. I did this willingly and without question. Seeing my family doctor always meant I left the office with a cocktail of chicken scratch on the prescription pad that included refills for Celexa, Senokot, Colace, Zantac, Domperidone, and Metamucil. This regimen altered who I was and how my body functioned in the world. I didn't realize the damage those pills and powders caused my body back then nor did I question what other options existed. I was on most of those medications for over four years before reaching my mental and physical breaking point.

When you grow up with so many firsthand encounters with Western medicine, hospitals, specialists, surgeries, and pharmaceutical medications, this simply becomes your world. I didn't know anything more existed beyond medical intervention and prescription medication until my mid-20s. Somewhere during my 26th year, something shifted. I began to trust my intuition more; an awareness came over me that the way I survived was not the only way there was to live. I started visiting natural health stores, researching herbs and vitamins, and learned about organic and free-range foods. I learned that there were options for my health and I wanted to know more.

Before I get any further, I want to be clear here. I am forever grateful for every single procedure my brother underwent and continues to, keeping his unique and incredibly complex body alive. Luckily for us, my brother was a fighter then and continues to be. Even 30 years later, he has beaten every doctor's prediction, every odd for survival, and still lives his medically fragile life with determination, purpose, and love.

But medical intervention was not the answer to my journey. What I truly needed back in my early 20s was support, understanding, and unconditional love for what I was going through and the story I lived. The many years of stress at home had taken its toll on me. What was more is that I carried a secret.

I was afraid that if I shared my deepest, darkest truth about who

I was, I would be shunned. When I came to terms with the fact that there was a name to describe the type of person I was and how I would show up in the world, it was both terrifying and liberating: I was a lesbian.

The first four years after coming out were some of the most heartbreaking and dark times in my life. Heading to the doctor for medication to deal with the ups and downs that presented at home, at work, and out in the world was what I thought was necessary and 'normal.' Thankfully, I chose my truth and my life path. My family eventually accepted the 'new' me.

Over the years, my self-confidence improved and I began living more naturally. I weaned myself off my antidepressants with the support of a naturopathic physician. I took homeopathic remedies and supplements that worked with my body's sensitive digestive system, out-of-whack hormones, and chronic constipation. I was living a healthy, active life once again. This involved eating clean, managing my stress pretty well, and pursuing my dreams.

But after my back injury and when I finally had an MRI and a diagnosis, I was once again faced with a decision of which route to go for my healing. As I sat across from my family doctor in December 2011, the conversation went something like this:

"So Kristy, results show you have two slipped discs in your L4 and L5 spine that are pinching your sciatic nerve."

"So now what?" I asked. "How do we fix it?"

"It's best you continue taking the anti-inflammatories and anything you need for pain. You're too young to go for surgery but if it doesn't go away on its own that's an option we can look into," was her response.

My heart sank in my chest. What did slipped discs mean? Could I heal myself? What about my career? What about my life? "These injuries can take a long time to recover, I'm afraid," the doctor said matter-of-factly.

I was informed but definitely not empowered. The options I was given not only frustrated me but left me in search of answers. I had two choices: go back to my old ways of pain medications and interventions, or continue a holistic approach to my health using food, mindfulness, and alternative medicine. I had learned so many tools, strategies and options for living a vibrant and natural life and I was determined that I could—and would—heal myself.

In January 2012, I stopped medicating altogether and began searching out new ways to live with chronic pain. I did not accept that surgery was even an option. I cleaned up my eating even further, adopting an anti-inflammatory diet and strictly limiting dairy, meat, wheat, and sugar. I consumed large amounts of organic celery, fish oil, and encapsulated my own turmeric powder. Although I noticed less pain from day to day with all the changes that I had implemented, it was six months into this new routine and something was still missing. My recovery did not happen to the extent I needed it to.

I hopped onto Facebook and put out a message asking my friends if anyone knew how to heal from slipped discs. There were plenty of folks feeling sorry for me and showing pity for my situation. Then, as luck would have it, an acquaintance sent me a private message asking if I had tried an inversion table. Two days later, she showed up at my door with the table in hand and said, "Keep it as long as you need. It saved my life."

I committed myself fully to the recovery process and ensured my routines reflected that. For six months straight, I inverted for at least 10 minutes every day, made my stretching and deep core strengthening a priority 3 to 4 days a week. I implemented weight bearing exercise using machines and nothing that required balance or agility. I went swimming, remaining buoyant as often as I could. I also started a mindset and basic yoga practice that brought the whole picture together.

Healing from slipped discs did not happen overnight. My healing journey took two years. It wasn't easy; I continued to have days where I wanted to give up. My ultimate goal was to wake up without pain and feeling back to normal, and not have to work so darn hard at it.

Things really shifted when I began to trust that my body wanted to heal. I told myself so every day using mantras like, "This pain is only temporary," and "We can and will get through this." I made a choice to rise out of bed each morning with positivity and purpose. I *would* fully recover and I was going to continue to pursue my love for fitness. I reframed my whole experience into a life lesson from which I was willing to learn.

It baffled me that I could suffer such a serious injury despite being so fit and strong. In time, I learned that the underlying cause of my back injury was a weak pelvic floor and overall core strength. Things like crunches, traditional sit-ups, and endless days in the weight room were not the answer to keeping my posture and core stability in check. This newfound knowledge led me to investigate and eventually specialize in pelvic floor and core rehab. Today, I am doing just that: sharing my passion and helping others regain their pelvic floor & core strength.

It was not until the 18-month mark that I hit a true turning point in my healing journey. I walked without pain, moved a little easier, and in that moment on that day, my faith in my body was fully restored. Instead of medicating myself with painkillers and anti-inflammatories, I used food, herbs, and supplements. Instead of trying to push through the pain and overdo it (which was my old story), I used yoga, stretching, and water jogging. More importantly, instead of surgery I used an inversion table, determination, and patience. I slowly restored my life and my body.

Just because you grow up with a certain set of beliefs, way of thinking and life experiences it does not mean you cannot shift your mindset and health destiny. Our minds have the power to overcome, conquer, and reprogram our thought patterns if we are willing to put in the work. That is exactly what I did by finding laughter in the face of fear and showing kindness toward myself in the face of defeat. Our bodies are magnificent and they are designed to heal, maintain balance, and function optimally when given the right support.

There is a time for medication and lifesaving surgeries. However, I challenge you to consider whether you need a counselor and more exercise over anti-depressants. Additionally, study the benefit of revamping your food choices and supplementation, instead of reflexively accepting a prescription. What's the root cause of your ailment? Are you willing to put in the time and effort to discover what will help you live your most vibrant life?

I believe that healing is possible for everyone. I believe it's the ultimate act of self-love to take care of our body, mind, and soul. When we do, that is when we really thrive.

Title:
From Doubt to Determination
Overcoming anxiety and injury through movement and
mindfulness.

About the Author

Kristy Ware

Strength Trainer, Nutrition Coach and Core Rehab Specialist.

Contact Info:
kristy@strengthandsoul.com
www.strengthandsoul.com
www.facebook.com/kristywarestrengthsoul/

Answer the Inner Call

Chris Kirckof

Sitting in my car in a parking lot of a doctor's office in the middle of nowhere South Dakota, I wondered how it had gotten to this point. A doctor just told me I should be taking an antidepressant. How could I have gotten here? I was a star athlete in high school. I was a college graduate with a master's degree. I had a good job. The answer was I had not been living the life I wanted and a toxic body and mind had now corrupted me.

At the time I was a physical preparation coach for collegiate athletes. My lifestyle mirrored what I saw in many of the student athletes. There was the appearance of health, vitality and functionality but that was far from reality. Eating terrible foods, consuming alcohol on a regular basis and overly excessive workouts created a mess in my body. Working a job I didn't enjoy and feeling the chains limitation caused a great deal of unhappiness. My body and mind began to work against me. I had severe joint pain throughout my body. I had frequent bouts of sickness ranging from common colds to digestive problems. My daily dose of antibiotics and pain medications did little to fix anything. I would lay awake restless until 4 a.m. most nights unable to fall asleep. When I did sleep it was because I knocked myself unconscious with medications. I felt fatigued constantly and my motivation to workout, see friends or even leave the house dwindled. I had thought I was healthy and happy but I certainly didn't feel vibrant. I had been lying to myself.

In that car was the moment I had an awakening. At that moment I finally saw the truth, no one was coming to save me. Until that very moment I had spent my entire life waiting to be saved. The answer to the question starts with realizing that the only one who can save you, is you. I started learning all that I could and I quickly discovered that much of what we are taught is simply untrue. I learned I knew a great deal about eating but little about nutrition. I knew more than most about supplements but very little about nutrients. I knew how to push my body in the gym but had no idea how to love myself outside of it. I had been looking outside myself instead of within myself.

Most people's entire day is just a routine of preprogrammed rituals designed to allow them to survive but never allowing themselves to thrive. They are going through life on auto pilot and are asleep at the wheel. They wake up and consume copious amounts caffeine just to get themselves feeling awake. They eat a sugary breakfast that doesn't even resemble food. They throw back some medications before heading out the door for a job that doesn't make them happy. The day consists of an overall feeling of apathy before they return home driving past the gym they stopped at once upon a time. They eat more unhealthy food at home and watch the television before drifting off to sleep only to repeat the cycle over again as if stuck in their own personal groundhog day. The term used to describe the way many people treat themselves is dysfunctional. However, people are not dysfunctional it's the social systems they live in. We experience painful and traumatic moments that can lead us into unhealthy patterns. A society that has produced the amount of sick, unhealthy and depressed individuals we have is dysfunctional. Worse yet, the system our society is controlled by is designed to disempower us and make us gravitate towards an unhealthy life. That is why laws are being passed to conceal which foods are genetically modified and which are not. It is also why you are constantly bombarded with advertisements for alcohol and temporary fixing medications that only treat symptoms.

Many of our corrupt social systems I have witnessed firsthand. I spent some time working at a hospital and I watched a man have a stroke because he was prescribed testosterone for fatigue, something it's not even approved for. I heard the dietician tell cardiac rehabilitation patients to eat foods that have been proven to cause heart disease. When I worked for a home that served people with mental illness and disabilities I saw them served the worst food imaginable and fed medications like they were candy. I listened to their psychiatrist change their medications and dosages like they were throwing darts at a dartboard. I worked as a personal trainer and had people pay hundreds of dollars in advance for training but then never show up. I have seen people who walk into the gym to earn insurance credit and then leave without ever working out. I worked with violent offenders who have been locked up for their crimes who live on a diet of sugar and psychotropic medications, both proven to cause erratic behavior.

Our entire world has become filled with sadness, stress, sickness and despair. At this point in time it is now rebellious to take care of your own health. The word "health" has etymological roots that define it as "wholeness." It is a being who is whole or sound. This does not just refer to the body but also the mind. The physical body and the non-physical mind interact with each other to encompass your wholeness. So when your goal is to become healthy, happy, and vibrant, you must consider what aspects of your life (body and mind) will need attention to bring your whole self into a healthy functional state.

The body is the most simple. It is your biological computer. This was the area where I disrespected my own self the worst. On the surface everything looked great. I had the lean muscle most men wanted, and I achieved great feats of strength in the gym, even setting several power lifting records. However below the surface a storm was brewing. I ate terrible foods and drank alcohol on a consistent basis. The consuming of artificial ingredients and processed foods that didn't even resemble real foods happened all too frequently. I had lost all respect for me myself and it's needs. My body became out of balance, which began having an impact on my mental wellbeing. I began by identifying the problems in my body and where they stemmed from. I began buying organic foods and rejected things with artificial ingredients. I removed sugar from my diet and I cut alcohol out of my life completely. I focused on better sleep. I began a workout program to correct imbalances and worked on weaknesses such as my mobility. I rejected all medications and found ways to address the root causes of my problems both physically and mentally. I learned the body can seemingly handle almost anything you throw at it, but that doesn't make it alright to treat yourself in such a manner. I look back on years of eating fast food, sugary treats, drinking alcohol in abundance and basically living in a state of perpetual chronic self-abuse. I consumed these toxic substances throughout my childhood and early adult life. The fact I lived that way and I am around living a life of health and vitality today is proof of the resiliency of human body. I often imagine how much healthier I would be if someone had just pointed me in the right direction and I had avoided the unhealthy road all together.

If your body is the computer, your mind is its hardware. Without this program functioning optimally the body will begin to shutdown. If this program becomes corrupted due to a toxic physical state, the mind can also cause the body to generate disease and dysfunction. Every second of the day your body is reacting and changing based on thoughts that run through your mind. It has been shown that just thinking about something causes your brain to release neurotransmitters that allow it to communicate with other areas of yourself. Your beliefs and thoughts also create your reality. Our beliefs manifest through our actions, but beliefs also communicate with our higher self in our physical reality. Thoughts alone can make someone happy, stressed, depressed and even diseased.

Not only had I been living in a toxic physical state but I also had toxic belief systems. My mind knew I wasn't being honest about how I had been living and treating myself. I had found myself at yet another job where speaking the truth and exposing the problems were frowned upon. This created a situation where I felt imprisoned in a self-created cell of frustration and powerlessness. Throughout all my different jobs I continually felt like I had to bite my tongue or I would lose the job, and I felt this was unacceptable because I was unsure how else to make a living. I watched as people where literally poisoned and fed lies that kept themselves stuck in an unhealthy and unhappy state. Due to the fear I held of speaking up I had betrayed myself and had created feelings of depression and despair. We may trick others into thinking we are satisfied but our mind forces us to notice our emotions through feelings of stress and sadness. Our energy life force flows through us, and when we block that energy from flowing freely, we up in a state of disease.

I learned that I had been operating from memory instead of imagination. The way we operate in life is a manifestation of what we believe. Like many people I had been operating based on my personal history, operating from memories of what I had done, seen, experienced and observed. My memory controlled my beliefs instead of my imagination. I believed I was unhappy with my life because I never operated from the idea I could be happy or accomplish what I wanted. I see this all the time with clients I work with who want to lose weight and improve their health. When most people think about their goals especially in regards to their health they focus on past memories or experiences. They begin having inner conversations with themselves convincing them they can't do it. Many times it's from the memory of failed experiences trying to reach their goals. Failed diet, lifestyle changes and workout programs of past flood their thoughts and operating from memory takes over from the imagination. The way you organize your mind and respond to your experiences and memories can either be self-abusive or healthy. I use specific meditation where I give more focus to my mind's activity. The goal is to become more aware of the themes, patterns and habits within your subconscious because those will illustrate the toxic thought patterns you will need to heal to create growth. By becoming more aware of my natural equilibrium I was able to identify things that took me out of balance.

As a health coach for many years I have witnessed firsthand how many address the problems on the surface without ever diving deeper into the subconscious underlying causes. I had people who came to me after going on crash diets where they starved themselves and spent endless hours in the gym only to regain the weight and usually more after it was no longer sustainable. This is no different than the clients who took pills to fix their mood or the person who drinks alcohol to forget about the job they don't like. They are temporary solutions or distractions from the life they don't want. All of this is the programming our society tries to teach us our whole life. Prepackaged ideas where someone else is pulling the strings and planning our movements and we are simply going along for the ride. If you are looking to increase your health and level up your life you're going to need to operate with new thinking and belief systems from your imagination and not your memory. Conformity and complacency run rampant inside our society. The idea that you should be just like everyone else is a major theme. That is why they aim small in their health and life goals and why some opt for medications rather than putting in the actual work to fix the root cause of the problems. It's the same reason why weight loss pills sell off the shelves and fancy workout gadgets that don't work sell for millions. Many don't want the truth or put in the actual work to make change, they simply have bought into the illusion they are doing something about the problem.

Take a look at your life. Are you satisfied with what you have produced? Would you like for things to be better? Do you believe you deserve better? Do you want to be healthier? Now is the time to start talking to yourself and start building yourself up. It's time to start encouraging yourself. Sometimes the only good things you will hear about you are the things you say to yourself. Quit looking around for someone else to build yourself up, it comes from within. Stop beating yourself up, over your mistakes, and stop talking bad about yourself. I know you've done it because we all have done it. It's become a natural inclination to put ourselves down. We are all born positive but we live in a negative world where we are taught and programmed to be negative and have feelings of unworthiness. That is part of the system of control to keep us feeling limited and powerless. It's time to listen to those inner voices telling you what you need to do and find your true authentic self. It's time to take the autopilot off and wake up. Once you wake up and honor your true self you will see the depth of the ways you give away your power away to others because you have perceived the source of what you seek to be outside of yourself. Once you access this inner power you will see that all your dreams are reachable and that you have all you need to make them become a reality. You will understand that your main obstacle has been yourself trying to sabotage you along the way. Each decision and moment in your life is a point where you can learn and know yourself more fully. We are each a work in development, letting go of what we no longer use and taking back what we lost. Begin operating out of a larger vision for yourself. It's time to operate from your imagination not your memory. Liberate your body and mind. You're best self is waiting and they can't wait to meet you.

About the Author

Chris Kirckof

www.soyouregoingtohaveababy.com
kirckofhealthyandfit@gmail.com

Your Dreams, Your Life— Realize with Real Eyes

Kelly Fisher

Hello, my name is Kelly Fisher. I have been a Certified Master Hypnotist for over 22 years, as well as a Certified Mind Coach. What I'm about to lay out for you is my personal study over my entire lifetime of how the mind works and how to get in control of your thought process to dramatically change your life. This is especially true when it comes to weight loss and completely changing the shape and look of your body. It has worked for me and thousands of my clients to live a more vibrant, healthy, and unlimited life!

The Six Building Blocks of Success

Building Block Number 1: Your conscious thought process is the only thing of which you are in 100% control.

Our conscious decision to make positive change in our lives is the only thing we can truly control. Everybody that struggles with life and their body image feel that life is coming at them and they don't know how to deal with it. The absolute truth is life comes out of you and you control your circumstances and situations. It's all about dialing in to the specific radio station and frequency of success. Of course, this is a lifetime of learning and is easier said than done, but still true. Give yourself credit for wanting change and finding the necessary resources to implement an improved way of life. Congratulations!

Building Block Number 2: There are 100 trillion cells in your body listening to your thoughts all of the time.

Why this is important for you to understand is because memory is held in all 100 trillion cells. That means when you're trying to break old habits, the fight or flight response, and what I call the Anxiety Circle, you have to realize that you are in conscious control of creating new habits and changing old ones. You will come to realize that your body and memory are listening. You must control your conscious thought for truly life-changing, dramatic results. One good practice tip is every time you look in the mirror, tell yourself how amazingly beautiful you are. This will feel like a lie at first. But after a short period of time, you will realize that telling yourself how ugly you are is also a lie. If you're going to use your imagination (to lie), you might as well use it for positive change.

Building Block Number 3: Thoughts create things.

Realize how powerful your thoughts are. Everything you see around you was once first a thought in someone's mind and imagination. Yes, this book you're reading, yes the chair you're sitting in—everything that reflects light at you and what you can see—was first a thought in someone else's imagination. That's how powerful your thoughts are. In this world of instant everything most people don't understand how this repetitive positive thought process works. After all, things don't create themselves.

Building Block Number 4: Thought—Feeling—Emotion

There is a very specific process that we are born with. Our thoughts create a chemical firing of the synapses in our brain and we instantly feel that thought, creating a chemical in the physical body that we emote out to the world. This system is important for you to learn because it is what our whole physical existence operates on. Get in control of this and get in control of your entire life. Just like Building Block #3 above, This IS how thoughts create things. THINK of great change in your life, FEEL (get excited) about that great change in your life, EMOTE it out, meaning get out there and do it!

Building Block Number 5: Perception vs Reality

These next two building blocks are little deeper in metaphysical study. Metaphysical just means, "that which stands behind," meaning the vibration that creates the physical. I want you to realize that I'm giving you the overview of how these laws of reality work. You perceive your so-called reality through the six senses. It means you interpret vibration on six different levels and call it reality. There is no objective reality outside of your six senses. That means everything you perceive as reality around you all happens because of your awareness to it. The best news of this realization is you are in control of interpreting all of these different levels of vibration into a life that only you can dream of! Create that internal vibration and see that vibration reflect light back at you! Thoughts become things.

Building Block Number 6: It's all vibration.

I know this is a quick rundown of the reality and life you are soaking in. But once you start to study vibration and the Law of Attraction, you will soon realize that these laws apply to everyone equally vibrating on this physical plane we call reality. The best news is we all have the same opportunity to change our experience on this physical plane. It does not matter where you're from or how you come; we all have the exact same tools to work with at our disposal. The only difference between the rich and successful, positive thinking people that are in great shape and living a vibrant life and you, is that they have studied and applied these laws to their lives and you have not. This is the great equalizer for every human on this planet. The best news is that now you have the knowledge of these laws of creation. Get excited about applying these laws in your life today!

Why You Don't Change

In the previous section, I laid out a blueprint of how to change your life in the most dramatic way. Study, understand, and learn to apply the six building blocks and your life will change dramatically. Now, let me explain the three examples of why you don't change.

Example Number 1: The story in your head is not you!

You have to understand and learn to separate the difference between the story in your head (that obsessive roof shatter, the yip-yip dog) and who you really are. This means there is you and then there is the story that's running inside your head like a movie. Unfortunately, the movie inside your head is just like what you see on the movie screen; you have no control over changing the movie on the screen. You can't run up to the movie screen in a theater and try to change what's being projected on it.

By the same token, understand that to change your story on the screen of your life, you have to go back to the projector and change the movie in order for the projection of your life to be different. In this example, the movie projector room is analogous to your subconscious mind. This means you have to learn how to shut off that roof shatter through meditation, and learn how to run a brand new movie in your mind of what you want your life to be. This is life changing! But you have to do the work, meaning you have to get into the practice every day for permanent change. (Yes I have meditations for this. Links will be at the end of this chapter.)

Example Number 2: The wake of the ship does not drive the ship.

In a brilliant Alan Watts example, he explains that the wake behind the ship is where most people focus their attention. Just like in the last example, most people think the story of their past drives their current situation and future. This is no truer than the wake of the ship pushing the ship forward. In this analogy, the wake of the ship is your past story, and past examples of who you think you are (the story in your head). You have to realize that looking in the rearview mirror is not going to guide your life in a new direction. You have to learn to face forward, grab the steering wheel, and guide your life exactly where you want it to be.

I know everyone wants to explain their past and defend who they are through this story. But you have to realize by doing this, it just holds you vibrationally in the loop of the old story. You could be factually right in explaining that old story and the old facts that happened in your life, but you will definitely not move forward in your new story. You cannot do both simultaneously. That is just not how focus works. Focus is vibration; you cannot play two notes (vibration) at the same time.

Example Number 3: You just haven't been taught yet how to grab the wheel.

Don't feel bad about not knowing this information yet. If no one has sat you down and told you how to refocus, retool, and take responsibility for your actions, then you simply have not learned this yet. The great news is you are learning this now!

The one nugget of knowledge I want to leave you with is the word *responsibility*. Most people feel that this word has a negative connotation to it. That's because most of the time it is a negative connotation in the law that you are responsible, meaning you are guilty of something. In the human development concept of life, responsibility is a very powerful thing. It simply means the ability to respond to any given situation while you are in it and with the most positive outcome that you can imagine. Taking back responsibility in your life means taking back your power. Yes, that means taking responsibility for the negative things in your life, too. The better you become at mastering responsibility and more aware you get of how this works, the faster you will see positive results in your life.

Imagination and being self-centered gets a bad rap.

Example number 1: Imagination

As Einstein said, "Your imagination is your life's preview to your upcoming movie." Just realize you're making all of this up. I had a client once ask me, "Am I just making this all up in my head?" My answer was "Yes, absolutely!" That is how imagination works. We make it up in our head first and then it turns into physical reality. We realize it in our imagination and then we see it with real eyes!

I was talking to a different client, telling him about my goals and dreams in great detail. Then I asked him, "Do you believe me?" He said, "Of course I do." I asked him why he believes me. It was because he believed I was going to do all of those things. It's interesting that he believed me because I just made all of that up in my head. The reason he believed me is because I believed in myself so much.

"Imagination is more powerful than knowledge. Knowledge will take you so far, imagination will take you everywhere." -Albert Einstein

Example Number 2: Self-Centered
In what point of our evolution did being self-centered and self-importance get a bad rap?

Here are a couple examples of how important it is to be self-centered and take care of yourself first.

The first example everybody knows but do not really apply it to their life in general. When you are on an airplane and the flight attendants give you instructions about the oxygen masks falling down, they always tell you to put the oxygen mask on yourself first. The reason they tell you this is if you try to help someone else first while you're passing out from lack of oxygen, you both die. You cannot give anything including oxygen from a position of lack.

The second example is if there were two people who couldn't swim and one was flailing in the water and you were on dry land. If you jumped in the water to save them, you would both drown.

The logical conclusion is you're standing on dry ground reaching out your hand saying, "Come this way. I can help you!"

The moral to both of these stories is that you have to be self-centered on dry ground, taking your oxygen first. Be self-centered, be self-contained, be full of life, and then you can help other people out of your abundance.

A.B.C. —Always Back to Center

One thing on your life's journey is that it's not IF life is going to throw you off center, but when. Your sole task is to work on getting back to center as quickly as possible. That means getting back to happiness, and regaining control of your life as soon as possible. All of your happiness and control are in the now (at center).

Again, this gets back to releasing the story of who you think you are. If your story is a negative one, it just means you will give more excuses of why you are off center and why your life is going so bad. When you have the realization that you can change your thought process in your mind and your physical vibration in your body to bring you back to the here and now without any holding on of the past, you will be back in control of your life.

That is your life's mission and everybody's mission vibrating on this physical plane. You have to realize (see with real eyes) to finally give up that old story rolling around in your head. You now know that you have the power to go back to the projection room in your mind, put in a new movie reel (real) and project it out onto the screen of your life. Take responsibility and understand that it's a good thing that you're responsible and putting in a new movie, projecting it out for everyone to see. Be proud of your decision making and be proud of projecting what you want in life for everyone to see. Everyone around you will respond to that in a positive way. I promise you this! As the saying goes, those that matter won't mind and those that mind don't matter.

How to Apply These Life Lessons

What do I mean when I say "realize with real eyes?" I mean that when you learn to slow your mind down to the speed you're living and meditate on the things you really want in life, your subconscious mind will project that imagination on to what most people call the physical plane (Maya) and actually create it in front of you. It is true manifestation.

Giving up on your story does not mean giving up on yourself. This scares a lot of people because even if their life wasn't that great, it's still their life. It actually means setting yourself free. I work with so many clients that believe they are the story inside their head and that they are the story from their past. They have this innate fear that if they give up on this story to move forward, they will lose who they are. Of course, my first answer is, "That is awesome! Let's give up who you were in the past because we are creating a new you for the future."

But you have to understand this is a huge paradigm shift for most humans. It is a pivoting point that separates successful people from those who want to hold on to who they think they are. The real question is which one are you? To have a new you, a new and different you, it means to have a major paradigm shift in your thinking feeling and reacting to who you think you are on this physical plane. Einstein's definition of insanity comes to mind: "To do the same thing over and over again and expecting different results."

Tying It All Together

Yes, this has to do with weight loss.

Yes, this has to do with changing your body image.

Yes, this has to do with living a completely vibrant life.

Yes, these are the laws of the universe.

Yes, you have to learn to apply these laws to dramatically change your existence.

Yes, it will work for you.

Yes, I am here to help you change on any level you are currently at. This is the blueprint to the universe. This is the map you will need to find your way home.

About the Author

Kelly Fisher

To get a copy of my current book:
Weight loss from the Inside Out: A Mind and Body Awakening
And my ground-breaking guided visualization audio program:
"Weight Loss Through Hypnosis"
Go to www.GlobalMindStretch.com

Also I have an amazing 6-week in-depth online training program called:
"Anxiety Solution" "Slow Your Mind Down to the Speed You're Living"
www.BestAnxietySolution.com

Also I have a program to help you fall asleep instantly at night:
Fall Asleep Instantly
www.FallAsleepInstantly.com

I have been studying my whole life on how the mind works. Of how we think and why we feel and how to interpret on all 6 levels of our perception. You can jump to the front of the line on this deep metaphysical understanding and have a very dramatic life-changing experience.

As always you can reach out to me at
GlobalMindStretch@gmail.com

All the best to you and your family.

"Whatever You Can Imagine, You Can Do...or at Least Attempt. Boldness Can be Magical and Freeing"

Tom Penland

Age may have some limitations, but your mind has so many more. As a Retirement Income Certified Professional (RICP®), I see my quest as one not only to help people plan sufficiently for the income they will need to live on in retirement but just as importantly, maybe even more so, to help them to think outside the box. Maybe even how to get out of... the "traditional" retirement box. The older we are the more precious life becomes. Living a life full of possibility is an option to retirement dullness. It is a choice. The value of almost everything is increased by its scarcity. We have always heard, "Live today as if it is your last." It is true for all of us that with each day, we have one less day, but this becomes all too clear in retirement. You can settle into the couch and call it a wrap or you can do, you can attempt almost anything. You can make your home stretch, the best part of your life.

You can make a difference (in your life or others) or you can make excuses. You cannot do both. Be bold. It is your last chance.

Live life full out. It is not too late. To be bold, you must start with confidence, courage, and direction, a focus. Little of real value comes without effort. As a matter of fact, the "effort" is part of the magic that can be freeing, rewarding. People who choose to be bold are inspiring not just because they get out of the box, not only because they do, they accomplish, but also because they instigate growth, progress, and movement for others around them. Sadly, far more people sit around watching the few be bold. They wish they would do something to shake things up a bit. Perhaps it's time to unleash the bolder you. You too can initiate, inspire and create magic and freedom in the process.

One action leads to another. Every step leads somewhere. Here are some things to consider adding to your daily actions, and see if some boldness, magic, freedom and who knows what shows up.

1. Bold retirees make acceptance a daily habit. Growing old is not for the weak of heart. That is why you must be bold. Accept your weaknesses, your flaws and then exercise your strengths to do everything you can, anything you want. Self-awareness is important. There is a difference between boldness and carelessness. Realistically acknowledging your limitations is one thing, but one thing it is not is making excuses to stay in the box. With age comes wisdom and with that wisdom comes the knowledge of when, where and how to take bold action and to know when you are out of your element. Boldness does not espouse danger per se. It does not necessarily even have to be related to something physical. Most constraints to boldness are mental not physical. Bold individuals minimize the risk of living out loud, for themselves and others by constantly reassessing and seeking partnership, the help of others to accommodate for any personal weakness. *Want to be a bold retiree?* Be more self-aware. Engage others who can complement your strengths and compensate for your weaknesses. The engaging of others also has its own and often big, big reward.

2. Bold retirees, have and maintain clear priorities. Jumping into action without a plan isn't bold. As a matter of fact, it will likely just prove to be foolish. Bold people know their objectives and prioritize them clearly. In retirement, we can maybe afford to be bolder than we ever have. It is your chance, your last chance. Now or never. Your lifetime's worth of experiences has prepared you to better recognize the right opportunity… to be bold about. You should be able to easier see these opportunities for boldness when they come along. *Want to be a bold retiree?* Know clearly what you want to achieve, what you want to do, where you want to go. Seek those chances, make the choices that will inspire and fuel a life fully lived. Avoid unimportant activities that lead to distraction. TV… argh. What could be more satisfying in your last days than feeling what I call 'action satisfaction'. You are OK to go on, to pass from here to wherever because you have wrung all the life out of life that you could. Each day is that opportunity.

3. Bold retirees speak up and speak out. I do not mean loud, boisterous, or obnoxious. I mean they have the courage to say something when it is important to say. They have the boldness to stand for something worth standing for. Your maturity will also lend itself to knowing when and how to say it so that it has the most impact. It is not being a bully or a loudmouth. Bold retirees must be better at tact and empathy, because the very nature of their words will carry power and impact. Bold retirees also understand and know when silence is the greatest statement one can make. They use it appropriately and therefore powerfully. *Want to be a bold retiree?* Say what needs to be said before your inspiration, your project, your intentions are derailed. Derailed by the naysayers, derailed by that little voice. Use silence powerfully, whether it is to make a statement or it is to focus. A quiet mind will allow for more clarity and that clarity will direct your boldness.

4. Bold retirees pair action with knowledge. Even though boldness inspires action, rashness should be at a minimum, maybe even non-existent. Retirement is no time to be rash! Remember, we do not want too many steps backwards at this stage of our game. But, do not allow fear to be construed as rashness. Understand and recognize the difference. Where there is too much fear there is no boldness. Bold retirees understand the power of knowledge, of learning and due diligence. Bold retirees want to be as certain as possible their actions lead to success. Therefore, they investigate first. They look before they leap. *Want to be a bold retiree?* Improve your odds of success by doing your homework. It will increase your confidence and your success rate, and your retirement satisfaction.

5. Bold retirees accept the value, and the power of failure. No one is totally comfortable with failure, but bold retirees understand that greater rewards come from greater risk, from the distance they are willing to travel from the proverbial "box" we put ourselves into too often, the 'box' society puts us in. Well, you know what? You can show them and yourself, otherwise. Bold retirees work to know how to use boldness, intelligently to their advantage. They harness the energy and the necessary mental chemicals, the adrenaline, and they do all that is possible to make certain that every failure is a learning opportunity. One that moves them up a notch on the boldness scale. They also know that even in failure, there is power, joy and even satisfaction in the action, in the "doing." There is immense value in the lesson learned. *Want to be a bold retiree?* Make failure an acceptable part of your process. Take the time to understand yourself, understand how to assess and minimize the risk. That way failure does not destroy, it builds. It builds even more boldness to try again, try something else.

6. Bold retirees make the most of small wins. Many people sit around and wait, they watch thinking somehow, some way, life will miraculously become more worth living. Then they will be willing to step up and take action, to live more fully. That is not boldness. Sadly, and rarely does life change in a way that makes it more worth living, more satisfying, more rewarding, more inspiring accidentally. Bold people understand that rarely is any plan for any project, any goal, or any mission perfect from the beginning. They look to make the most of any given set of circumstances and resources that can lead to success, to a sense of accomplishment and satisfaction. Bold retirees know that it can be the little wins, the first steps towards anything that add up to a journey worth taking. *Want to be a bold retiree?* Start with a small hurdle you are confident you can get over, map out a plan, and take the field. Getting over the first hurdle breeds confidence and leads to the next hurdle. Furthermore, by seeing you trying something new, watching you get over each hurdle will undoubtedly inspire another. Maybe it is another retiree, maybe it is a child or grandchild, maybe a stranger. You have no idea who you may inspire, or what they may accomplish. You have no idea how it could ripple out well past your time here.

7. Bold retirees build momentum. Bold people recognize that a single accomplishment is just that. They ask what is around the next corner, what else do I want to do, see, accomplish, complete? If they don't know, they ask themselves, now what, what is next? They work to create a series of actions that help them to build even more confidence, clearer clarity, and effective actions. They develop an instinct for efficiency, effectiveness. They know when to push, whether themselves or others, have a sense of when to add energy to advance the ball and when to let the momentum carry things for a distance. *Want to be a bold retiree?* Craft your retirement 'actions' plan, your roadmap of boldness, if you will, so that each action takes advantage of the previous success. Take advantage of any win that adds peace, joy, contentedness, respect, satisfaction and value. Do not be surprised, as I inferred above, if you get noticed. You may become a retirement light, to show others the way out of retirement grayness, away from the TV, and into their own life worth living. Allow this to add fuel to your momentum. Retirement is probably the best time to 'give back' and love it. Activate those that notice you. Share what inspires you, be willing to cultivate those new and valuable relationships. No one knows what is possible. Create excitement for yourself and you will undoubtedly create something for someone else too.

8. Bold retirees are gracious at heart. This in turn makes them nice, makes them humble. They find reasons to be grateful every day. They count their blessings even in adversity. Retirement brings its share of challenges and difficulties. More than some, fewer than others. But with those challenges can come growth and opportunity. By seeing these challenges with the right (grateful) attitude you will move further down the path of retirement joy and accomplishment. Remember, our thoughts become our reality. What you "see" is what you get. Even after complete loss the bold are willing to reinvent themselves. They find reasons to get out of bed and they find and acknowledge the things they have to smile about. Those times of failure, and even loss have the power to make us sensitive to and grateful for the blessings in life. We can all find reasons to be grateful and bold retirees seem to make an extra effort in that category. It may be the people who love you, good health, wonderful memories, the bills being paid, or just the chance to laugh. Bold retirees share their appreciation with those who support them, past and present. BE BOLD!

I appreciate the opportunity to write about the "other side" of retirement. The non-financial side. In addition to being a retirement planner, I am the local chapter president of Adult Financial Education Alliance. I teach at the local community college and library. My courses are of a financial nature and I teach people how to squeeze the most out of their hard-earned money... with certainty. I do not believe that when it comes to your money, you can afford to be bold. Bold usually means taking risk, and along with monetary risk can come loss. In my opinion retirees cannot afford to lose what they cannot replace, financially speaking. I find and advise that making the most of what you have saved, once you are no longer earning is the better, safer approach. I enjoy teaching. I finish every course, every class with the same ending, "In the last days of our life we are not going to be wishing we had more money. We are going to be wishing we had more time. More time to spend with people we love, more time doing the things we never did, helping those we never helped, so retire as soon as you can comfortably do so."

As the founder and CEO of a retirement planning company, I would like to end by sharing our "GREEN CODE" in an effort to give you an idea of what we are up to at GREENLINE ASSOCIATES. The foundation of everything we build upon at

Greenline Associates is the Green Code—a 12 point design that not only guides us, but also reminds us to be the very best we can be, for ourselves and for others.

1. We are never complacent. Each day offers the opportunity to start fresh. A chance to reinvent, evolve and adapt for ourselves and for our clients.

2. Our mission is to protect and care for your hard earned money. Money is the harvest of your work and paramount to freedom.

3. We are fair. We treat everyone the way we want to be treated.

4. We are always learning. Every experience, each exchange is a chance to become wiser and to become better at what we do.

5. We learn from the past, take action in the present as we anticipate the future. We are motivated by what can be done today so that we may be better tomorrow.

6. We listen as a way to simplify. We must "really" hear our customers to keep our communication clear.

7. We are always asking why or why not. The only thing that cannot be improved upon is our mission.

8. By creating value for others, we create wealth for ourselves. Growth and profit are the proof that we are accomplishing our mission.

9. Only the truth can be upheld. Without trust there can be no real relationship, no progress.

10. We are each our own person and together we become more. The only thing needed to be our customer is your independent thinking and determination.

11. We are not here to conquer or dominate. We are here to instigate and initiate. To be "a" choice...is the way we are designed. Competition is healthy. We are not enemies.

12. We will go on forever. Anything begun with integrity, having an honorable purpose, carried out with boldness and dedication will go forth in ways unseen.

About the Author

Tom Penland

Thomas Penland, RICP®, is the founder of Greenline Associates and a Retirement Income Certified Professional with over 30 years of experience. He volunteers time as the Torrance Chapter President of AFEA and has taught more than 1500 registered adult students through classes and workshops at El Camino Community College, Los Angeles Harbor College, and other locations around the South Bay.

To get a copy of my current book:
Risk Less Spend More: Everything You Never Learned About Retirement

Contact me at: www.greenlineca.com

I Seek Therefore I Become

Matt Clark

I remember waking up in hospital with the doctors around my bed. The first word I heard from them was, "Whew!" I realized then that it was a lot worse than what I had originally thought. The previous months had been intense; I was going to the bathroom 20 to 30 times a day, regardless of whether I had eaten anything, and had lost a lot of weight. I went from 82 kilograms down to 59 kilograms in a space of two months. There were stages where I was so exhausted that I couldn't even get out of bed, didn't want to eat anything for fear of having to go the bathroom another 10 times. I went from being strong, healthy, and fit to skin and bones. It was pretty scary. I used to have a great butt and then it was non-existent, to the point that it hurt to sit down on a cushion because I was literally sitting on the bones. The doctors had diagnosed me with Crohn's Disease. (I don't like giving it a name because then you give it power, but now you know what they called it). There were a couple of times that it was touch-and-go and my family, friends, and doctors weren't sure of the outcome.

I had tried herbologists, nutritionists, naturopaths, specialists, driven halfway across the country to see a guy who apparently knew how to fix me, went to practitioners that did blood tests and would prescribe natural medicine (one of which I called a snake doctor), yet no one seemed to have an answer for me despite all the promises. The medical doctors didn't have an answer for me and all the others said they could fix me, but instead of getting better, it became even worse. In fact, there was one time where the doctors wanted to take out my colon and give me an ileostomy bag. I absolutely refused to be cut open, no matter what.

Despite all of this going on, I knew that I was going to be alright. There was actually one specific moment when I knew I would be okay and it was right before the worst moment I experienced. I was sitting in the waiting room waiting to be admitted for surgery. When you have this challenge with your stomach, it can cause horrible sores close to your exit, and I needed to get it surgically repaired.

I sat in the waiting room and saw something that completely overwhelmed me with emotion. A group of kids in hospital gowns no older than 10 following a nurse. None of them had any hair. I realized they all had cancer and were undergoing chemotherapy. I had an overwhelming sense of sadness and then gratitude. I was so grateful at that moment that I only had what I was going through and it could have been so much worse. My heart just went out to them. They had no idea, but they had given me the strength to get through anything that was coming my way. There was still more to come.

Over the next couple of months, there were a lot of ups and downs but more than anything, I learned a lot about myself. My biggest lesson was that no matter how much support I had, no matter how much love surrounded me, no one could go through what I was going through for me. No one could go through the pain for me, no one could fix me for me. I had to do it myself. That was the real start of my healing journey.

I was on an incredible amount of medication. it seemed as though everyone just threw all sorts of medication at me to see what stuck. I spent an incredible amount of money on medication that didn't work. I was also doing a lot of my own research and what became abundantly clear was that there was no clear fix for the condition that I had been diagnosed with. I had to find another way that didn't include doctors or medication. I read an article by Louise Hay that said stomach issues are a symptom of holding on to past experiences and emotions. This struck a chord with me and I decided to explore further. I went to spend some time with a friend of mine who is a hypnotherapist and we started peeling back the layers, unravelling the past and started letting go—and man, was there a lot to let go! There were experiences and emotions that I thought I had dealt with but they came back with such force that I knew I hadn't truly dealt with it.

At the time, I was also running my business and expanding internationally, so I had to think about things differently. (I'll get back to that in a second because this is a big part of living a vibrant and abundant life for me.) I met someone who had been incredibly successful in business and he taught me one of the most valuable and powerful exercises. It is called the forgiveness exercise. Before I went to sleep every night, I would forgive everyone for everything. Sometimes it would take five minutes and other times it would take an hour as specific instances with certain people would come up. Once I had forgiven them, I would then forgive myself. For things that I've done, things that I hadn't done that I should have. Pretty much anything that came up where there was an emotional attachment, I forgave myself and let it go.

I believe that when you ask the universe for something with love in your heart, it delivers. For me it delivered someone that helped me really break through, in fact it's another author in this book—Ed Strachar. Read what he has to say again.

He taught me that in order to heal, I needed to truly love myself. When you have been through what I have been through and look in the mirror and to see skin and bones, one of the hardest things to do was to look at myself and love myself. But I forced myself to stand in front of the mirror every day, looking myself up and down, filling my heart with love, and telling my reflection that I love myself. This is one of the key things that I learned to live a vibrant life. It changed my relationship with myself, my friends, family, business associates, and clients. It made the relationships that much stronger. I started vibrating on a higher frequency. I became unafraid to tell people how I feel because I realized that it's not about how other people feel; it's about how I feel. I found that when I truly love myself, I am vibrant and the right people feel it and are attracted to me.

This leads me to business, because it is something that I am passionate about and love helping people to succeed. Before I went through this experience, I had a company that I was completely bound to. I made incredible amounts of money, but I had no freedom and poor quality people in my life. I had no time and all the money in the world couldn't make it enjoyable under those circumstances. Now don't get me wrong—I like money. It makes living a vibrant life so much more fun because of all the awesome things you can do with it. But money is a tool; it does not define me and is not the end goal.

I knew I had to create something better that would allow me the freedom to do the things I want to do and complete the circle of what it means for me to live a vibrant life. I decided to build a company where I could travel the world, experience the people and culture, and learn from others in completely different industries without having to worry about work all the time. I had to think about business completely differently and had to come up with a way to achieve this so that I could have tons of fun, make great money, help a lot of people to achieve more freedom, and live life on my terms.

I created a company that specializes in automation and online marketing with the mission to elevate the level of business worldwide. My mission is to help people connect with who they really are and in turn connect to their ideal client, reaching them no matter where they are in the world. When I work with people, I take them through a learning process to gain clarity and connect with who they are, showing them a better way of doing business and how to expand their reach by using online marketing automation.

When I see the results people get, I become even more excited that I am on my purpose. You see, I get to teach people the lessons I have learned, help them create more freedom, money, and live their life on their purpose—really connecting with them on a human level. Most of the people I work with wind up becoming friends and we create opportunities together. When I saw what automation brought to my life and my business, I went all in. It allows me to focus on what I really love to do and have the time to connect with the people that are in my life and the new relationships that form.

If I can sum up what I have learnt and experienced in four points it would look like this:

1. Love yourself unconditionally no matter what you look or feel like. This will allow you to love others the same way.

2. Forgive everyone and yourself. It's not worth carrying any of it around with you. Let it all go.

3. Realize that you are responsible for your health and healing, wealth, and happiness. No one can or will do it for you.

4. Build your business so that you love it and can have the life and freedom you desire. Automate as much as you can.

Go build the life you deserve!

About the Author

Matt Clark

Having built multi-million dollar companies, I know that being healthy and vibrant is what makes life worth living. For me, there is no difference between personal life and work. I believe that we are surrounded by opportunities, and those opportunities present us with choices. I choose to be happy and prosperous every day. To automate my business so I can travel the world, engage with incredible people and fully enjoy my life. To grow and to prosper so that I can help others live their purpose. The most exciting thing is when I see my clients start to think differently and actually achieve their dreams and break free from what is 'normal' in business and life. Do you want to be next?

Connect with me on any one or all of these platforms:
Email: matt@thevirtualedge.com
Facebook: www.facebook.com/mattclarksa
LinkedIn: www.linkedin.com/in/mattclarksa
Website – Living: www.thevirtualedge.com

How to Live a Vibrant Healthy Life

Karen Jones

Everyone has the same starting and ending point in life. What happens in the middle is your story! The choices you make may be similar to others, yet the outcomes are different due to individual circumstances. Following someone else's plan does not guarantee you will receive their results. You have to find what works by trial and error. When you figure it out, honor your body and how it responds, staying on course for optimal results.

Research studies show the fastest growing segment of the population are centenarians. This number is projected to reach 6 million by 2050. Studies have revealed the happiness factor increases longevity. When you live with joy, gratitude, and focus on your life today (rather than on missed experiences of the past), your happiness increases while decreasing the rate of illness.

Today, everyone wants the quick fix solution: *Just tell me what I must do to shorten my journey and accelerate my success.* The choices we make on how to live our lives are filled with either purpose or chance. The formative years are full of guiding habits and behaviors. Beyond that, the journey is to make your life what you choose. There's only one person guiding you on this journey: YOU!

Now is the time to wake up and come alive! Here are the three keys to living a healthy lifestyle: let go, embrace change, and have fun.

First Key: Let go.

Remember roller coaster rides when you were child? Do you recall the anticipation of waiting in line and feeling the butterflies in your stomach until it was your turn to get in the car? Do you remember deciding if you wanted to ride in the front of the coaster, or were you courageous enough to ride in the car solo? When the ride starts, the brave ones raise their hands and ride the roller coaster without holding on. Everyone screams and you enjoy the exhilaration of letting go!

If you've never been on the ride, you may feel butterflies beforehand as you aren't sure what to expect. You hold on to the safety bar or are courageous to say, "I can ride and let go of holding on." Life is about giving yourself the pleasure of letting go to enjoy the ride even if you're not sure how it's going. You can be courageous to enjoy the ride outside of your comfort zone. Alternatively, you can be hesitant and hold on, or skip the ride altogether.

Letting go is about all the stuff in your life, both the physical and emotional things you hold on to. What happens to your attention when you're feeling overwhelmed and pulled with conflicting situations? It's because you're suffocating from things that are in your physical and mental space. It feels as though everything else is consuming your precious oxygen. When you're able to let go of the physical or emotional baggage, you'll notice how your lungs expand and you can breathe easier. You even feel lighter. When you remove the physical clutter, you'll see the additional space you create. Amazing as that sounds, clearing out the clutter has benefits.

What does creating space in your life mean? When you have so much in your way, you're bursting at the seams and can't move. The memories of experiences that weigh on your mind are additional weight on your shoulders. You can release the pain of these experiences by changing your current beliefs. The belief you have about this experience limits you from releasing it. Even your muscles hold onto the pain of the past. By revisiting the experience in a safe environment, you are able to release the past, forgive yourself for carrying this burden, and create a belief that supports you today, rather than one you created when the episode occurred. When you release a past experience that holds you back, you're creating space for new positive experiences. Letting go is acknowledging your past instead of feeling stuck in a painful moment. You move through the healing zone to enjoy new experiences.

Second Key: Embrace change.

Is there something in your life you want to change? A few examples may include starting an exercise program, changing your morning or evening routine, changing your eating habits, eliminating something you know is affecting your health, or reducing the stress in your day. How often do you face a situation you want to change? It feels more challenging than expected.

Making a change is difficult. Understanding how to move through it to make it manageable is about reprogramming yourself. You can change habits and behaviors with repetitive actions over a period of time, such as 60, 90, or 120 days. When the changes are made for a few days, the results are less sustainable. That is because it's easy to revert to the past routine without much thought. In order to make a change, you must reprogram your brain out of following the motions for a minimum of 60 to preferably 90 days or more. For most people, change causes discomfort. When you reframe the change as the key to your personal development, there is a personal benefit. Making a change recalibrates our focus on how to be a better person. Being challenged and uncomfortable is expected when you face doing something different. No one admits it will be easy.

There are ways to address making changes easier. Do you have a hobby or a favorite activity you enjoy? Are you energized as a result of the activity? A hobby is a special skill introduced to you as a child. It may have been a bonding time with a family member, parent, or grandparent. It could be gardening, woodworking, completing puzzles, painting, singing, dancing, sewing, crafts, photography, fixing things, or making jewelry. The possibilities are endless.

Hobbies are an extension of your comfort zone; they are soothing and feel good. When you view the hobby as a way of taking care of yourself, you can feel a sense of curiosity, creativity, and adventure. The longer the individual period of time you experience the hobby, the more grounding it provides. You feel nurtured from the hobby and can use it to propel you to go outside your comfort zone to make changes. For example, as a result of the creativity you feel from woodworking or painting, you are energized to feel creative to focus on a change you want to make.

The personal development experience from embracing change focuses on taking care of yourself. Change is the lever tapped to create different experiences in our life. Change is having the ability to impact your surroundings, your personal perspective, and finding what provides personal joy or happiness when you expand beyond your current experiences.

By embracing change, I encourage you to take a few deep breaths, stretch, and be courageous for the adventure you will discover as a result. Your personal growth confirms embracing change is meant to be repeated throughout the years.

Third Key: Have fun.

When you think of fun, what is the first thing that comes to mind? Playing games, having a party, being happy, doing silly things, connecting with your inner child, and celebrating. It's ironic that in our goal driven business world, the focus is heavily weighted on achieving the results rather than even taking a few moments for a congratulatory celebration or for the journey that achieved the results.

Some adults say there isn't much reason for celebration. Meanwhile an acknowledgement of a job well done is reason enough to celebrate; you feel appreciated and the recognition feels good. As parents, celebrating is a regular activity for rewarding children for their efforts. Children are motivated by the celebrations and acknowledgements they receive. (They even insist on continuing these celebrations.) Unfortunately, these reinforcements usually stop after grade school. Either parents run out of energy or they delegate the celebrations to others.

Adults benefit from celebrations, too—probably more than we realize. Some adults who have not been recognized for their achievements continue to look for acknowledgement in their relationships, sometimes creating a point of contention. When we connect with those around us and focus on improving our relationships with communication, we have fun and celebrate with the people in our lives. But having fun is about celebrating every day, acknowledging our achievements and expressing gratitude for the good things and abundance in our lives. When we show appreciation, our gratitude expresses our sense of joy.

Do you take the time for having fun and celebrating? Having fun is letting your inner child out and expressing joy. Everyone enjoys fun to lift their spirits. Without the fun, every day is routine and going through the motions is monotonous. Having fun is about the increasing the joy in our lives.

Yes, having a vibrant, healthy life is about the three keys which enable you to process the past and let go, living each day in the present and celebrating your life. It also incorporates daily nutrition and exercise, but it's much more than that. It's about getting the rest your body and brain require to heal from your daily activities. Spending time outdoors and getting exercise also contribute to a healthy lifestyle. Everything in life is about balance; all the areas of your life are linked together, so when one area is deficient, it affects everything else.

Our choices are an expression of who we are. The choices we make are critical to our personal growth, celebrating who we are, and why we're here. Relationships are the connections with others and are also critical to your well-being. More importantly, your number one relationship is with yourself. Designing the life you desire is possible when you look within for the vibrant, healthy journey you create.

About the Author

Karen Jones

Karen Jones is a holistic coach and transformation guide for corporate professionals unfulfilled in their careers, and resistant to the next step in their life to wellness (personal and professional). She authored, *Let Go, Embrace Change and Have Fun, Living the Joyful Life You Design.* She's Founder of KScopeFocus.com and speaks on the Healing Zone and taking care of yourself.

She's experienced the rollercoaster ride when her marriage ended unexpectedly, and two years later she became an empty nester. After 17 years in corporate Human Resources, she became part of a corporate downsizing. She looks at change as the wake up adventure in life to take care of yourself.

Contact Karen directly at Karen@kscopefocus.com, or call (480)800-9155.

Pain and it's Gift of Personal Transformation

Ron Ario

My wish is for my story to capture your attention, that somehow it will trigger a realization of the vast potential and unlimited nature that is you. I hope my story inspires you to questions you may have overlooked, such as: Why am I here? Where did I come from? What is the purpose of my existence? Is there a greater meaning to my life I have not considered until now? These questions make up the fabric of our existence, whether we are willing to acknowledge them or not. To the degree that we give value to these questions, the realization greatly determines our overall joy, happiness, and fulfillment in life.

I would like to take you through a summarized version about my life's journey. It will take you through tragedy, accomplishment, breakdown, and breakthrough. At various points, there were obstacles and self-imposed limitations, but also how I went from the victim to victor. While this is my personal story, there will be relevance to yours as well. What's important is not in comparing each other's stories, but the humanity that we share together in our pursuit of true happiness in this human form. My goal is to enlighten you about our true nature, which expands far beyond the social conditioning and programming that blinds us. This story demonstrates that your pain is not only a gift, but a path leading to personal transformation.

I was raped at the age of 6. The event was so traumatic that I immediately blocked it out of my mind. This psychological trauma set the stage for a life path that provided many accomplishments and eventually the destruction of each of them, so that I would have another mountain to climb. Inside, there was this deep, black hole that always threatened to swallow me whole. The only way to escape was to distract myself with seemingly impossible tasks. Once I mastered one thing, I'd set up for another—constant distraction was numbing and exactly what I needed.

I was also born hearing impaired, as was my whole family. Career expectations were non-existent and working for the union pension was perceived to be the highlight of personal achievement. Not getting hearing aids until I was 19-years old proved challenging as well: I continuously shied away from social interaction to avoid embarrassment. Sports were my savior in my younger years, and I thrived from early on. Excelling from little league to high school basketball, from schoolyard baseball to the semi-professional league. I also excelled in professional soccer as a goalkeeper, having never played soccer until the professional level. As long as I had sports, I didn't have to feel the darkness inside. I figured that if I just kept moving and feeding my distractions, all would be okay. I gave professional soccer a shot until subsequent injuries ended my run in 1983.

The reality of an overachiever with a career in sports soon gave way to a real estate career. I had such an inferiority complex about learning prior to studying for my real estate license that I sought a hypnotist to help me with my confidence in order to pass the test—which I did. I started working as a licensed real estate agent in March of 1983 and made three sales in that same month. Soon after, I quit the labor job I had taken after giving up professional soccer because by October of that year, I had accumulated 19 sales. I never looked back after that. For the remainder of the 1980s, I was a national top producer. Sports weren't my distraction any longer; business was, and it was perfect.

In 1988, my failed marriage led to the loss in motivation for real estate sales, and I needed another big challenge. A family member entered me into a California US Man of the Year contest and I was accepted. There were several months before the contest began, and because I was petrified about going up on stage, I took acting classes to boost my confidence. Acting was my greatest fear because I had created this persona, an image I wanted the outside world to see. Deviating from this persona—a person who had it all together, good looking, in great shape, and successful—would show my true vulnerabilities. I didn't want this to happen, but told myself that if I could accomplish acting, then I could accomplish anything in life. Within six months, I had my first part on the soap opera, *Days of Our Lives.* Soon after, I landed a series of 40 small parts on the soap opera, *Young and the Restless.*

I juggled real estate in between acting jobs, and soon life responsibilities insisted I focus on business full time. In the late 1990s, I wanted more of a leadership challenge, so I took a marketing position in the largest real estate servicing firm in Southern California. I expanded this company from a regional business to a nationally recognized firm in just 18 months. It was here that I discovered my gifts for leadership, teamwork, and innovation. However, I was competing with the owner for leadership and my exit was written on the wall.

I then took on a position that nobody else believed in, but I saw the vision: Regional Director for Keller Williams Realty in the Central/Southern California Region. Nobody knew who Keller Williams was, but I knew there was a future for a real estate company that took learning to the next level. I grew that region to 14 offices and 1,400 people from 2002 to 2006. When I saw that I had made the owner of that region very rich, I wanted it for myself.

Fortunately, I partnered with CEO, Gino Blefari of Intero Real Estate Services. I became the CEO and Master Franchisor of all of Los Angeles County in late 2006. It was my perfect distraction and potential life fulfillment. Six months after I acquired Los Angeles County for Intero Real Estate Services, the biggest real estate crisis—since the great depression in the 1930s rocked the real estate industry. Most of us just survived for the next several years. For me, the business that had served as a distraction from the darkness that entered my life during early childhood was now fading, and it didn't seem like it would not be revived anytime soon.

Because of the Great Recession, businesses shut their doors left and right. By 2012, restlessness began to grow inside of me. Like most, I only focused on the external world, never anything inside. I began to see the injustices in the financial industry and the unnecessary wars that crippled humanity. So, obviously, I wanted to save the world. I needed something big, something impossible, to keep my focus and attention.

I launched WORLD PEACE 2012 in an attempt to blanket the world with peace. The idea was based on the quantum theory that if enough people think of the same thing at the same time, a shift in the collective consciousness can occur. I was asked to give the keynote speech about world peace at the Los Angeles Convention Center on July 6, 2012. The event was an economic exhibition for Cote d'Ivoire and several other African countries. My keynote speech followed the ambassador to the United Nations for Cote d'Ivoire. Following the event, an audience member contacted me for humanitarian projects but it soon fell through. Finding something bigger than saving the world did not exist, and my personal world came crashing down. The combination of physical, mental, and emotional pain led to a profound spiritual crisis.

In March of 2014, I did 14-day water fast. My goal was to get to the bottom of what was haunting me. Shortly after the water fast, my reality began splitting at the seams: I became conscious of a spiritual ascension as I experienced a swift spiritual growth and rude awakening. Still, I was not prepared for what was to follow.

I awoke at 3:30 a.m. one morning. As I stumbled towards the bathtub, I began to relive the traumatic event that happened to me when I was six. I experienced it physically, emotionally, and mentally all over again. I screamed so loud that it woke the neighbors. Once I finally saw the truth, I can honestly say I was relieved and honestly grateful. I had suspected some things, but not to that magnitude or level of pain.

After that experience, I also came to the realization that there was spiritual contract that this individual and myself had. I saw how my whole life was designed to bring me to this pivotal point and how this person had agreed in spirit to carry the burden of doing such an act to a young boy. I also saw that this life was truly an illusion: that there are no victims and we truly do not die--and cannot die. We are energy beings and our souls are infinite and timeless. We have existed for eternity and will continue to do so. This was the catalyst for my spiritual awakening.

Immediately after that, I sought to forgive this individual. I did not want to hold any anger or contempt toward this person at all, and felt like I had had enough of it throughout my life already. I set aside time in my morning and evening meditations to forgive this person. They say the highest act of forgiveness is to thank the person for the act. Of course, this is easier said than done. One day in meditation, I went deep: I connected my heart to this person's heart, sending love from my heart to theirs. I did it from my soul because I wanted to be free and live completely pain-free, too. In an instant something came over me and my heart began to expand, continuing to do so until the love that flowed out of me became overwhelming. Tears flowed down my face as I experienced true compassion and forgiveness.

I experienced myself beyond this illusion of form, it consisted of an unconditional love for myself and others that was humbling. It was such a powerful feeling that I never wanted to end. This was the beginning of my awakening. What I would like to share next is the magic of living within this heart space.

In the spirit of living a vibrant life, I would like to share all the beautiful gifts I have gained from having an extreme life that included my own share of pain. Pain is subjective and all pain is relevant. I read Eckhart Tolle's *The Power of Now* several years ago. I liked the concept, but couldn't apply it in my life previously. But now I can and I do.

Pain is a gift to our life experience until we wake up and have no use for it anymore. Without pain, we would not seek the deeper meanings and answers to our existence. Most people cannot experience the present moment as they live in their head, constantly reliving the past and fearing the future. When life exists in the mind, the present cannot be appreciated or fully enjoyed. Pain is like a vice; if it squeezes hard enough it literally renders the mind helpless. But when pain is strong enough, the gift of this *now moment* presents itself, and you cannot escape it. You must either deal with it directly or lose your mind. Thoughts slow down as you observe them. The gift lies in this experience because you can see this moment is pregnant with your thoughts and emotions.

Your reality is birthed only in this omnipotent, present moment. It is in this moment that you experience a direct manifestation of what you think and feel in your physical realty. You come to realize that you have always had complete control of your life experience; it is all dependent on how you choose to respond. If you respond to life with love and beauty in each present moment, then life responds in kind. Your life is simply a reflection of your eternal present moment.

Now, this is not something one can master right away. You will have many tests along the way. The more conscious one is of their personal response to life's circumstances, the more beautiful life becomes. If you want a life of beauty and peace, one that lacks drama and pain, then consciously respond with love, beauty, and peace.

Our pain in life is not the circumstances we're presented with. Instead, our pain is our attachment to the outcomes we expect in life. When we lose our attachments to outcomes and stay present, pain has no choice but to retreat. When we accept that we have created all present moments and that they return to us for transformation, we begin to master our lives. We begin to master the process of transformation where authenticity takes a front and center stage.

First, being authentic with ourselves and accepting our human frailties opens the door to authentic relationships with everyone we encounter. Once we fully embrace our authentic self, a door opens to self-compassion that naturally extends to others. We are not only transforming ourselves at this point, but others as well. We become living examples of our greatest potential: our divine essence in form permeates our human existence. We recognize we are energy beings, as this energy is now tangible in our lives. We clearly see that we are multidimensional beings existing in this human form as well as experiencing our soul's existence beyond.

Living a vibrant, healthy and happy life is about taking complete responsibility for our life experiences and outcomes. We remove the label of victim and understand that we are spiritual beings that have come to the planet for a reason. Each of us has our own mission and purpose; no one is more important than anyone else. Our lives, our spiritual contracts, and experiences exist to simply awaken us to the deeper, more profound aspects of our multidimensional selves. But all these are not without pain. Pain is nothing more than a gateway to experiencing our highest potential. There is no awakening without pain because pain is the onset; the dark before the dawn. This is the path to fulfilling our personal mission.

It takes courage to feel everything inside. Just know that you are the observer and director of your life's experience. You are a spark of divinity imbued with the omnipresent knowledge of creation itself. My wish is for you to see that anything and everything can be overcome in this life regardless of the circumstances. We are all victors by virtue of our soul's existence. Our souls are ageless and timeless. It is time to awaken from this grand illusion. The time has come to awaken to who you truly are!

About the Author

Ron Ario

Contact Information:
310-844-8999
+63-949-652-9924
RonArio11@yahoo.com

How to Loose Weight and Get Healthy: Inside Secrets

Jason Christoff

If you're confused about what it takes to lose weight and get healthy, you're in good company. There are more books available on health currently than at any other time in human history and oddly enough the public at large (no pun intended) are sicker and heavier than ever before. What's going on? Is there something we're missing regarding how we're supposed to stay healthy? The answer is yes. Our society is missing one very important piece of the puzzle and it's time the public found out the truth about why it's so hard to dedicate full time to living a healthy lifestyle.

What the public isn't told is that the foods we embrace or ignore at the grocery store are related to safety and security based relationships we developed during our childhoods. You can't change the foods you eat unless you fully understand why you pick the foods you eat. Let me explain.

When we were growing up, we understood very quickly that much larger human beings were charged with the task of raising us. Our parents are large and we as children are very small. This large difference in power initiates the child mind to use what ever resources are available, in order maximize our own personal safety and security. Even as children our minds and nervous systems are fine tuned to the evolutionary task of survival. One survival mechanism adopted very early within all children is the act of bonding with our large human caregivers (our parents), in order that we build and maintain the relationships we need to survive. One of the easiest ways to bond with anyone (including our own parents or guardians) is to mimic that person's behavior and habits. The psychology, in this case, is very easy to understand. If a child acts and behaves like their parents, the parent is more likely to admire and bond with that child, based on the simple fact that most humans instantly gravitate toward mirror images of themselves. The human ego thinks very highly of itself and when it finds another human acting in the exact same way, the attraction and bond is instant. Humans generally think they're awesome and so by extension, anyone acting exactly like them is most likely awesome as well. That's the way the ego operates. Children recognize this trait in the human ego and take full advantage. A child's mind is hard wired for survival in this manner, regardless of age.

In short, we mimic the behavior of our parents, including their dietary habits and their levels of self care. I remember one of my clients named Mark. Mark's father was a cigarette smoker. In order for Mark to forge quality bonding time with his father, Mark took up smoking at a very young age. It was obvious to me (as an experienced health coach) that Mark's smoking was based on mimicking his father's behavior, in order to establish a safe bond with the patriarch, because Mark saved all his cigarettes for when his father got home from work. Mark's Dad took a real shine to his son because Mark acted and behaved just like he did.

Mark's Dad also ate unhealthy food, his level of self care and self maintenance were obviously very low plus Mark's Dad also consumed a couple alcohol based drinks after work every night, binge drinking reserved for the weekends. Mark unfortunately mimicked all of this (and then some), in order to achieve the maximum level of safety and security available during his highly unstable childhood. The father figure, regardless of situation, is the protector and safety provider for the child. The closer a child gets to the father figure, the greater the bond and therefore the greater the safety that child will feel inside an often unsafe and chaotic world. The more scared the child, the more aggressive the mimicking of their caregivers. How humans mimic as their primary formed of learned behavior is brilliantly explained by Santa Clara University psychology professor, Jerry Kroth, inside his lecture titled, "Propaganda and Manipulation."

After Mark moved out of his parent's house, he still kept smoking, even though he was old enough to take on the role of "protector" to himself. With the unhealthy habits of smoking, junk food eating and binge drinking firmly under his belt…Mark's health started to fail. This was inevitable. Mark's not magic, as no human can bypass the consequences of a self abusive lifestyle. If you consume poison, you get sick. No health professional on the planet knows what exactly will break first but when you poison yourself, something's going to break. That's a guarantee. All those years dedicated to self attack and self destruction were now coming full circle for Mark.

Even with death knocking at the door, there was a part of Mark's personality that was petrified to lose the bonding rituals he had worked so hard to forge with his father. There's a reason that all psychiatrists and psychologists eventually rock back in their chairs and ask, "so tell me about your parents?"…because we are our parents on almost every level. This very pressing "change or die" scenario that Mark was facing plays out so much in our society today, that no one really gives it the attention it deserves. I assume many who are reading this are facing a similar dilemma.

If you personally are having a hard time being healthy, day in and day out, this mirror imaging of our parent's habits is most likely a major factor. Although you may have tried and failed to be healthy more times than you can count, by understanding how the human mind really works, you can maximize your chances of success if you happen to try again. Allow me to explain what it took for Mark to turn things around.

I've brought you now into the territory of self sabotage. A phrase that means, "I'm unable to live the life I really want because I'm too busy living the life I don't want." Mark knew he had to change in order to save his own life, as many in our society today also know, but there was some invisible force shackling him to the habits that were destroying him. Deep inside Mark's psyche (inside his child ego), he was afraid that if he showed up healthy to his childhood home, he would be rejected because no one in that household was healthy. What Mark needed to become, was the exact opposite of everything he already was.

The fear of societal, parental and peer group rejection was guiding Mark's hand to the junk food at the grocery store instead of the organic vegetables. As Mark entered the grocery store, his mind would look at the junk food and equate such poison with safety and security. This psychologically based magnetic attraction to the wrong choices, set up a perpetual manifestation of Mark's worst life. When Mark would see the organic vegetables and the other healthy food selections, the same part of Mark's mind would equate the healthy choices to fear, panic and rejection. This was the invisible force driving Mark into the abyss, thus guaranteeing him an eventual painful and premature death unless he could break free of this self sabotage cycle.

Although it's highly illogical to be provided freedom of choice and not to use it to save yourself, this is what was happening to Mark and of course it happens to millions inside our society every day. Our encoded human psychology is getting the better of us. Saying that, there are documented methods that can help us get the better of our psychology and make peace with our inner saboteur.

This is when I sat Mark down and explained to him what was driving his self abusive, self destructive, illogical and irrational behavior that clearly lacked any self care, self love, self maintenance, self worth or long term planning. I had to very carefully enter Mark's personal heart space and psyche, where many land mines were waiting for any intruder. I had to get close to the love that he held for his father, without setting off one of those land mines, which would have had Mark turn away before I could initiate the healing process.

I explained to Mark that self sabotage was about two phrases. One phrase is, "what used to save you, now starts to kill you." Although Mark survived a very traumatic and chaotic childhood by using perpetual self abuse to gain acceptance and approval with his father, those rituals of self attack and self destruction were now killing him. In order for Mark to survive, he would have to leave his addictions behind and morph into the real adult that he was always destined to be. In short Mark's addiction and unhealthy lifestyle were blocking his ascension, evolution and maturation process.

Mark would have to graduate to father, guardian and protector of himself and he would need to be confident enough that he could fulfill that role in his own life. I explained to Mark how to use healthy food and healthy living principles to gain the immense energy reserves he would need to make this transition. The energy we need to make this quantum leap emotionally can only come from healthy food and healthy living protocols. This type of transition is in fact the birth rite and destiny of every human being on the planet. A transition many people are avoiding simply because our society sells self serving, self indulgent, pleasure seeking as its foundational living philosophy while discounting painful rites of passage that make us more comfortable in our own skin and that allow us to take on our true adult roles within the tribe.

The second phrase that I use to describe self sabotage is one that I've hijacked from Marshall Goldsmith, which is…. "what got you here, won't get you there." As Mark and I sat down, I had to explain to him again that it was now time for him to change and take a knee in front of his child self. I told him to picture his 5 year old self, scared and needing reassurance. The 5 year Mark was small, eyes to the ground, frail, in need, weak and shaking. This boy was Mark years ago and our scared child selves still travel with each of us. "This is your hurt inner child Mark", I explained, "and he's still terrified of the world because no real adult has ever been there to care for and protect him."

Although Mark had a father, no child can be calmed and truly protected by anyone, unless that person is a true adult. What qualifies as a true adult though? True adults link long term. True adults think 5, 10, and 15 years down the road. Children think 5, 10 and 15 minutes down the road. Real adults don't smoke, drink, or eat junk food etc because all those activities reflect short term self pleasuring outlooks. A real adult is a true protector and they consider the family or tribe first, not just short term personal pleasures. I was inside Mark's heart space now and proceeded with extreme caution before explaining that it was time that a real adult started to care for Mark's hurt inner child.

I asked Mark one question, "Who do you think this new real adult is supposed to be?" And Mark replied, "I see what you did there. It's me who now must care for the young scared version of myself." I then told Mark, "...you have one shot at this. Don't break trust because real adults never do. From this moment on you must be the adult that calms your hurt inner child, only thinking long term, putting the tribe and the family first. Never break trust with your hurt inner child and be the leader you were always destined to be. Kneel down to look eye to eye with your 5 year old self and open your heart. Put your hand out gently and ask for your child's hand. Look your child in the eye and declare with strength and confidence that it's time to move forward and that the future is safe. Stand up and walk hand in hand with your hurt inner child into a safer and secure future together. No one is left behind. And in your own mind you must swear to all that is good in the world that you'll never under any circumstances allow a real adult to leave Mark's side again... ever. With this ritual you are now an adult to yourself, your hurt inner child and every other member of the tribe. Rise up to the man you were always meant to be. Rise up and finish your journey with passion, confidence and strength."

Mark's eyes got a little glossy, which showed that his heart was opening and that the healing had started. This small seed of healing is now growing and this rite of passage, the transition from a boy into a man, will take hold of every cell in Mark's body. My job was done.

Mark now started to go over to his parent's house without fear, fully understanding that he was the leader and true adult in his life. He stopped smoking, quit drinking, started exercising and developed enough self love, self worth and self care to grab an organic vegetable without feeling that he would lose the love of his Dad and the family. What was also surprising is that when Mark started to show up at his family home bringing organic whole food selections to family events, his parents had already prepared their own healthy selections in order to make him feel welcome and loved.

As Mark tabled the bravery to heal, he in effect started a wave of healing throughout his own family and beyond into his peer group as well. His parents loved him unconditionally and relied on him as much as he loved and relied upon them. It was extremely important that Mark took on the role as leader and protector in his own life, which was always his destiny, because a couple years later......Mark's Dad passed away. Mark then took his place as the healthy adult and strong leader in the family, taking care of his mother and many other family members during that time. A real adult is the only cosmic force that brings peace and stability during times of extreme chaos and emotional upheaval.

You can't change what you eat and how you live until you understand the "whys" behind what you eat and how you live. If you're having a hard time getting healthy, losing weight or leaving childish behavior in the past (where it belongs) maybe Mark's story can help you understand the invisible forces that keep us stuck in our stuckness. Maybe it's your time to participate in this ancient rite of passage, to fulfill your true destiny? Maybe it's your time to take the hand of your hurt inner child and be the adult you were always meant to be? One life. One time at bat. Swing for the fences. Push the prison door open. You'll find it was never locked. Live a healthy life today. As we heal ourselves, we heal the world.

About the Author

Jason Christoff

Jason started Physical Limits Fitness in 1994 at the age of 24, after graduating from McGill University with a degree in Labor Relations. He has written over 1000 health articles, with hundreds appearing in many newspapers across Canada. Jason has been interviewed recently by several US radio stations regarding his principles on healthy living. Jason was also invited to speak on health topics on The CBS Morning Show and also appeared briefly on the Dr. Phil Show featuring fitness trainers from across North America. Jason is currently writing a book tabulating the steps that he used to lead a healthy and addiction free life.

Jason specializes in exercise coaching from the CHEK Institute, functional stretching, self sabotage, healthy living principles, overcoming addiction, weight loss, healing while facing a health crisis and small business start up consulting. Jason believes that health is about developing habits based in self love and self respect, as a way to propel one through life in a successful way. You can contact Jason through his website at www.jchristoff.com, on facebook or directly at info@jchristoff.com.

Living a Healthy Lifestyle

Robby Besner

The earth provides us with everything we need to live a vibrant, healthy life. Spending time in nature is proven to have a positive effect on overall health, physically and emotionally.

Here comes the sun!

Just a few minutes of exposure to the sun, or nature's vitamins, not only makes you feel better emotionally, but it also contributes to your physical wellbeing, reducing blood pressure, heart rate, muscle tension, and produces anti-stress hormones. Sunlight is one of the best natural ways to re-energize and revive the body. Within the wavelengths of the sun resides the safe, full-spectrum infrared frequencies. These energies are known to stimulate, heal, and nurture the body. When I think about the single most important health enhancement that can make a significant difference in the way you feel, I always come back to sunlight and the infrared spectrum within a ray.

Good vibrations come from nature's infrared wavelengths!

The study of infrared energy and its applied sciences has turned out to be my life's pursuit. Twenty years ago, I stumbled onto infrared frequencies and their many health benefits while searching for the best protocols to help heal my daughter Julia, who was diagnosed with Chronic Lyme disease. I was looking for a natural method to give her relief from body pain and extreme toxicity. Infrared's gentle wavelengths penetrate seamlessly into the body because they harmonize, or resonate, at the same frequency as water inside the body. Healing starts at the skin level and can penetrate as much as three to four inches into the body. Each wavelength, or frequency, has a very specialized therapeutic effect and can truly set a wellness platform fundamental for optimal health and feeling good.

Don't believe everything you hear about the sun!

The politics of sunlight drive us away from the very thing that can save us. We are strongly influenced to believe that sunlight is harmful. Furthermore, scaring us by explaining that the sun's rays are solely responsible for the significant rise and multitude of skin conditions and cancers because our atmosphere (the ozone layer) has been adulterated, allowing harmful rays to enter our atmosphere and our lives. There's always a shred of truth clouded by obscurities designed to confuse us (and even worse), frighten us into shying away from the natural energies gifted from the heavens to nurture and heal us.

Water is a primal key to good health.

Dr. Gerald Pollack, considered one of the world's authorities on water, revealed in his book, *The Fourth Phase of Water*, that sunlight, particularly the wavelengths within the infrared spectrum, restructures water inside the body. This by itself is fundamental to sustainable wellbeing and improves cellular communication and function. Dr. Pollack tells us that in his clinical studies, healthy, thriving individuals all have one thing in common: the water within their body is structured and in proper order. Natural sunlight is the most efficient way to achieve this.

These specialized sun energies also change the electrical charge of the body, creating a grounding or "earthing" effect. When water is energized by infrared frequencies, it becomes the most bioavailable water for essential cell function and health.

Negative ions—positive vibes!

Negative ions are another one of nature's miraculous gifts. It's critical that our body has a balanced electrical charge to support a strong immune system, improve efficient cellular communication, and neurological connectivity. These charged particles occur in nature from the earth; when environmental friction affects water, (like at a waterfall, when the waves hit the shore, or when rain comes through the atmosphere) to free up an electron, (which has a negative charge) to marry and balance with a positive charge (your body). It turns out that the earth's charge is negative, hence the term "earthing." Just as the sun gives us warmth and Vitamin D, the earth gives us food and water, a surface to walk on, and a natural, gentle energy, and sound frequency—otherwise known as Vitamin G for grounding.

When your bare feet come in contact with the earth, free electrons are absorbed into the body. These electrons, nature's antioxidants, help neutralize damaging excess free radicals that can lead to inflammation and disease in the body. Bringing more negative charge into your body improves your overall health down to the cellular level and makes you feel better! Our bodies quickly respond to negative ions (or negative charges) that instill a sense of wellbeing and euphoria, making you feel happier. I don't know about you, but I can always use a larger dose of happiness in my life. Even just a few minutes of exposure to infrared wavelengths and negative ions help change your body's electric charge.

The ultimate in anti-aging!

The reason why we age is because of something called oxidative stress. When we're young, our bodies make specialized signaling mechanisms that target and soak up free radicals, balancing the delivery of oxygen to our tissues and cells. These are called redox molecules. As we age, we make less of these antioxidants so the body cannot handle the flow of oxygen to our tissues as efficiently. Guess what? Sunlight, specifically the infrared spectrum, initiates the production of these most needed redox molecules again, thus slowing down the aging process. Bathing in the right kind of light turns out to be the fountain of youth!

Technology can be harmful!

In our modern world, we have insulated ourselves and our own energy fields from nature's frequencies and the earth's energy fields by spending most of our time indoors and in front of blue screens and smart devices. Many of today's technical advantages and lifestyle conveniences, though important, also contribute to the energetic imbalances that most of us harbor. What you can't see can hurt you! Exposure to EMFs (electromagnetic fields) is another paramount environmental stressor to the body that lowers your immune system and exacerbates many health challenges.

It is important to recognize and implement simple choices to limit the body's exposure to these harmful fields that disrupt our natural rhythms and impact us physically and emotionally. You don't really expect companies that manufacture these devices to tell you about this or protect you from the short-term and long-term effects of these man-made energies, do you? We can't stop socioeconomic advancements, but you can learn about them and find simple, inexpensive ways to protect yourself and your children.

Does it really matter what diagnosis you have?

Isn't it more important how vibrant you feel? To me, it's all about my energy level and being free of symptoms that might slow me down. Mostly, it's about my ability to live my life to the fullest. By the modern definition, "Health is a state of complete physical, mental and social well-being and not merely the absence of disease or infirmity." The key here is living symptom-free and living purposefully. Wake up and be enlightened by the healing benefits of nature!

The formula to a healthier lifestyle:

Rule #1:   Follow Nature's simple lessons.
Rule #2:   Listen to what your body tells you about your health. Notice everything!
Rule #3:   Take charge of life and you will take charge of your health!
Rule #4:   Follow Rules 1, 2, and 3.

Get back to the basics:

- Get grounded. Go to the beach, walk barefoot in the sand. Above all else, take your shoes off!
- Walk in the grass or hug a tree. Connect with the charge of the earth and its vibration.
- Get more natural sunlight, particularly the afternoon sun when the healing and infrared spectrum frequencies are most prevalent.
- Reduce your exposure to electromagnetic fields. Look for ways to protect yourself and loved ones from overexposure to harmful EMFs.
- Pay attention to the messages your body gives you.
- Eat organic if you can. Beware of and try to avoid or remediate the treacherous amounts of environmental toxins in our food, water, and air.
- Bring more oxygen into your daily life by practicing easy breathing techniques or go for a 20-minute walk.
- Improve your sleep.
- Understand that everything you read or hear is not necessarily true or in your best interest. There are socioeconomic influences that negatively impact our short and long term health. Look for simple solutions to protect yourself and your family.
- Detoxify, physically and emotionally.

Easily incorporate nature's healing energy with infrared and negative ions into your life with simple and affordable solutions!

There is a variety of devices that can be used to bring infrared wavelengths into the body. For full-body bathing in infrared frequencies and the best natural detox, there is the traditional wooden box sauna. The important thing to note is to make sure it is made with natural, non-toxic wood and materials. Also, consider what range of frequencies are generated and if the unit produces harmful electromagnetic fields.

Portable infrared saunas have taken over the playing field. They are much more affordable, take up less space, are versatile and portable, can be used in the comfort of your home, and allow you multi-task while you detox. These are the most popular and preferred by many in the healthcare industry. With your head outside of the unit, you can accelerate the heat without overwhelming the brain, so you do not run the risk of off-gassing from amalgams in your mouth and diminish the possibility of inhaling your own toxins as you detox. These portable units deliver all the benefits, and in some devices, offer much more than the traditional large wooden models.

Infrared heating pads are another great way to bring the healing attributes of infrared directly to the body. These can be used to soothe muscles that need TLC, pain relief, de-stressing, or can be applied to an organ that requires localized detoxification. Here again, use many of the same criteria for device selection, understanding that whatever model you choose, all of the attributes apply, including the best practices for optimal results.

Reduce your exposure to harmful EMFs by maximizing lifestyle choices and invest in simple and affordable natural shielding products. You can easily check in with your energy medicine health professional to get fine-tuned applications that will best serve you and your family.

About the Author

Robby Besner

For more information on our infrared products, please contact us at:
Therasage
Email: info@therasage.com
Website: www.therasage.com
Call us: (888) 416-4441

5 Simple Steps to Achieving Peak Mental and Physical Health

Patrick Porter, Ph.D.

The most dangerous health epidemic we face today is what I call 21st Century Super-Stress. It's a worldwide crisis and is the result of the fast-paced, high-tech, over-stimulated lifestyle that everyone is leading in this new era of total connectivity and never-ending access to media hype.

Stress manifests itself in physical maladies—many of which have also become new millennial epidemics—such as ADHD, obesity, diabetes, insomnia, migraines, autoimmune disorders and high blood pressure to name but a few. But what's happening at this time in history that has never occurred before?

When we're under stress, our bodies pump out adrenaline and cortisol. This reaction is a natural part of your body's defense physiology. Your sympathetic nervous system—often referred to as the **fight-or-flight response**—is a mechanism your body employs to keep you safe from injury or attack. The problem with our modern world is non-stop over-stimulation that traps us in sympathetic overload and eventually becomes Sympathetic Survival Syndrome, which means your body stays in sympathetic overdrive, even when you're trying to wind down or fall asleep.

When you're stuck in this highly-aroused state, there is no room for creativity, exploration, or contribution to the world. Only when, or if, your body returns to a state of homeostasis can healing take place. In other words, your body must have recovery time to achieve peak states of mental and physical health.

More than 2 billion people worldwide currently suffer from brain-based health challenges

All forms of stress, whether it is stress about a relationship, time, job, money, or emotional stress, are a form of brain stress. We've become so accustomed to this lifestyle that we don't even realize the damage it's doing to our mental and physical health. The reality is that we cannot escape the fast-paced, high-tech, high-stress lifestyle of the 21st Century, so we must learn new ways to deal with the stresses of life to prevent it from causing problems for us, both physically and psychologically.

Still, you might be wondering: *How can stress make us physically sick? How do emotions wreak havoc on our bodies?*

Stress isn't just in your head. It's a physiologic response to a perceived threat, whether that risk comes from an attacking lion, or from running late, an overdue bill, an argument, or constant exposure to email, CNN, and Facebook.

When you're stressed about anything, your body responds. Your blood pressure and pulse rise. You breathe faster and more shallowly. Stress hormones flood your bloodstream, which your body must deal with later. When you allow yourself to stay chronically stressed without a recovery period, all these changes in the body can lead to health problems such as high blood pressure, ADHD, obesity, cancer and more.

What you need to know about stress

There are three different types of stress, and only one of them is inherently bad for you.

First, there is *acute stress,* that natural reaction of the sym-pathetic nervous system I've already discussed. Acute stress is geared for survival and protects us from danger. Under normal circumstances, once the threat is gone, the body settles back into its usual routine. No harm, no foul.

But then there's *chronic stress*, which is a different animal altogether. It's the stress that builds up day in and day out. It's the daily grind of long commutes, money woes, an overbearing boss, or difficult co-workers. It's the type of stress that can significantly affect both your mind and body. Common signs of chronic stress include irritability and anger, anxiety, depression, headaches, poor sleep and a sluggish memory.

Chronic stress shouldn't be taken lightly. It has far-reaching effects on you both physically and mentally. Fortunately, there is another form of stress that can help reverse the effects of chronic stress and provide you a happier, more productive life.

Discover the beneficial form of stress that can get you whatever you want in life

Fortunately, there is a good kind of stress that can be a powerful motivator in your life. It's called eustress, and it can help you achieve your goals, enhance your performance in work or sports, and provide you a general sense of happiness of wellbeing.

Consider competitive sports as an example. The more excited the athlete gets about performing on the field or court, the better he or she does. The intense pressure competitive athletes are under galvanizes them into peak performance in a way the rest of us can't fathom.

But here's the key to determining which form of stress manifests for you: **It's your *perception* of a stressor that controls which kind of stress you experience!**

Take a non-competitive athlete and put him or her in the same high-stakes situation and you'll quickly see eustress turn to distress!

The trick to using eustress to your advantage lies in your perception of the task at hand. If you have an upcoming high-stakes game, exam, or a project with an impending deadline and you respond with negative emotions, you have set the stage for procrastination, poor performance, distress and unhappiness.

Conversely, if you choose to get excited about meeting the challenge, or focus on the accolades you'll get for your accomplishment, you will engage the power of eustress—triggering your brain and endocrine system into a state of peak performance and setting the stage for you to become a high-energy, peak-performer with an excellent quality of life.

It's all in your focus

If you want to develop a eustress habit, the first step is to shift your focus and get re-centered. To succeed at anything, you must first see yourself succeeding. Given that visualization involves seeing what you want with the added benefit of repetition, it's the perfect tool for changing your perceptual filters, especially when it's done through technology-enhanced meditation such as the BrainTap Pro app provides. There's no better way to manage your perceptual filters and use eustress to your advantage.

I challenge you to take advantage of the technology-enhanced visualization sessions in my free trial of the BrainTap Pro mobile app. To try them out with my compliments by visiting: **www.braintaptech.com/free-trial**

Now, let's get started with your 5 simple steps to achieving peak mental and physical health!

Step 1: Breathe.

The next time you're relaxing comfortably, take a minute and see how your body feels. Think about how you breathe when you're relaxing before sleep at night. Taking full breaths brings your body into homeostasis where you can rest and recover from stress.

Deep breathing is one of the best ways to lower stress in the body because it sends a message to your brain to calm the body and relax. The detrimental effects of stress--such as increased heart rate, increased stress hormone production and high blood pressure--all decrease as you breathe deeply to relax. I think proper breathing is so important that I include it in every guided visualization I create.

Read the following paragraph and then close your eyes and follow the instructions it contains:

> *Take in a deep, cleansing breath. Hold that breath for the mental count of three and then let the breath out with a sigh. Just let it go. Let go of the thoughts, the cares, the concerns of the day.*
>
> *There's absolutely nothing that needs to be done right here and right now. The only thing that really needs to happen is for you to relax and let go. Now take another deep breath. Hold it for the mental count of three, and then let the breath out with a sigh.*

Did you feel your body let go of the stress and tension with each deep breath you took? Did you feel your muscles relaxing as you imagined yourself letting go of the stress and strain of your day?

Creatively visualizing a space and a place where you can breathe in deeply and breathe out completely, relaxing and enjoying a peaceful, quiet time is vital in letting go of stress and anxiety and allowing rest and recovery for your body.

Step 2: Focus on the Moment

When you are stressed and anxious, you're most likely regretful about something you've already done or worried about what comes next. These negative thoughts can cause vast amounts of stress from which your body needs recovery time.

One way to lessen this type of stress is to bring yourself back to living in the moment. Be mindful of what's going right now. If you're walking, feel the sensation of your legs moving. If you're eating, focus on the taste, smell, and sensation of the food you're consuming. If you're relaxing, be mindful of the heaviness of your limbs and the deep, rhythmic sound of your breathing.

Mindfulness allows us to just "be," which is a state associated with relaxation. When we are always going and doing and reacting to past or future events, we are continually exposing ourselves to stress. Being in the moment allows us to relax, heal and tune in to the needs of our bodies. You will find that you can deal with situations that arise positively and productively because you are reacting to what is, not what may have been or might be.

Step 3: Reframe the Situation

When we are stressed or overwhelmed, it may seem impossible to find a positive in the situation, but one of the best ways to attain our peak mental and physical health is to remain positive, especially in the face of stress. Viewing stressors as opportunities can help you stop feeling trapped and reduce the physical effects of stress. And it's really not as hard as you think.

Let's look at an example:

You're running late for work and then find yourself stuck in traffic. Your usual go-to response would be getting upset, stressed, maybe even cursing or yelling at the traffic around you.

It's important to remember that not only does this cause a rise in your body's stress level-causing muscle tension, blood pressure and hormone production, which leads to disease in the long term—it's also not going to solve the present problem. You can't do anything to change the situation and, therefore, getting upset is pointless and detrimental to your health.

Take a different perspective. This traffic jam is allowing you to have a few extra minutes to yourself, which is probably a rarity. You can listen to the music on your car radio, get your thoughts organized for your day, or enjoy some quiet while you wait for the traffic to clear.

So how can we reframe any situation? Look at the steps below to turn your next bad day into a day of possibilities:

1. **Look at what is actually stressing you.** Rather than dwelling on the feelings of frustration and helplessness, examine the situation with new eyes.
2. **What can you change, if anything, about the situation?** Think of as many solutions as you can, without judging right away if you can or can't do them.
3. **Look for the positives.** If you're in a situation you genuinely can't change, you can reframe your thoughts and change the way you feel by finding benefits in the situation you face.

4. **Find the Humor.** Have you ever been in a situation that really was so terrible that you thought, someday I'll look back on this and laugh? Why not let someday be now?

Step 4: Keep Your Problems in Perspective

The next time you're feeling stressed, consciously make an effort to think about the things for which you're grateful. It's important to remind ourselves of the positives in our lives--we woke up this morning; we can see; we can walk; we have family and friends to support us. You'll find this a surprisingly easy way to reduce the stress in your life.

When your thoughts are positive, the body responds, and the brain seeks to find the most favorable outcome for any situation. When you focus on the negative or find yourself caught up in the stress of a situation, you can only see adverse outcomes, and the body responds with the fight-or-flight response, triggering the high blood pressure, increased heart rate, shallow breathing, the release of stress hormones and more.

Stress happens when we don't feel capable. When we stress over bills, it's because we don't believe we have enough or can't get enough money to pay them. When we stress over a relationship, it's because we don't feel capable of making the relationship work out healthily.

Thinking positively means that you don't ignore that there are possible negative outcomes, but you focus on the result that you want and, like superstar athletes, step up to the challenge with optimism.

Step 5: Practice Mindful Meditation and Creative Visualization

There is a growing body of evidence for the role visualization and meditation play in achieving peak mental and physical health. Visualization directly influences the body by calming the mind, slowing breathing and heart rate, and relaxing muscles, creating the optimal environment for mind/body balance and radiant health.

By practicing mindful meditation and creative visualization, such as by using the audio sessions in the BrainTap audio library, you can learn to achieve the relaxation response. The relaxation response is a physical state of deep rest that changes a person's physical and emotional responses to stress. Once you enter the relaxation response, the brain sends out neurochemicals that neutralize the effects of stress on the body. You immediately experience the benefits of lowered blood pressure, lower pulse rate, lower respiratory rate.

The creative visualization sessions offered in the BrainTap audio-library are neuro-encoded™ to help you reach the relaxation response and at the same time develop the characteristics of happy, healthy, prosperous people who enjoy meeting life's challenges head on instead of stressing over them. By practicing mindfulness and visualization in this way, you can reduce or eliminate brain fog and negative mind chatter, rid yourself of unwanted habits and behaviors, have more energy, relax and develop positive sleep habits, gain memory and focus, and improve the quality of your life.

A message from the author:

Since the mid-1980s I've been testing, using, and researching the science of light and sound frequencies for deep relaxation, visualization and peak brain performance. I believed then, and still, do, that brainwave entrainment technology should be in the hands of every individual, and that, if it happened, our world would be transformed instantly. I've made this my goal since the day I first encountered this remarkable technology, and it's the reason I developed the most advanced brain training system to date.

But you don't have to take my word for it. You can experience this life-altering technology for yourself as my gift to you. You'll have access to a series of my guided visualization audio sessions, all of which I have neuro-encoded™ with tones for brainwave entrainment and peak brain performance. You can start experiencing all the benefits outlined in this chapter beginning today. www.BrainTapTech.com/free-trial.

About the Author

Patrick Porter, Ph.D.

Patrick K. Porter, Ph.D. has been on the cutting edge of brainwave entertainment technology for 25 years. He was a co-developer of the MC2, the first personal light & sound brainwave training machine, voted "Best New Gadget of the Year" at the 1989 Consumer Electronics Show.

His newest device, BrainTap, is distinctively designed to take the Brain Tap Technology sessions to the highest possible level with the addition of light & sound frequencies.

Dr. Porter is known for developing Positive Changes, the largest self-improvement franchise using mind-based technology, making him a highly sought-after expert within the personal improvement industry. Dr. Porter's successes were featured in *The Wall Street Journal*, *Business Week*, *People*, *Entrepreneur* and *INC magazines*, as well as ABC, NBC, CBS and the Discovery Channel. He is a licensed trainer of Neuro-Linguistic Programming and is the head of mind-based studies at the International Quantum University of Integrative Medicine (IQUIM).

He is the author of seven books including: *Thrive In Overdrive, How to navigate Your Overloaded Lifestyle* and the bestseller, *Awaken the Genius, Mind Technology for the 21st Century*, which was awarded "Best How-To Book of 1994" by the North American Book Dealers Exchange. Most recently, he co-authored with Dr. Bob Hoffman, *Your Flourishing Brain; How to Reboot Your Brain and Live Your Best Life Now,* a book that teaches chiropractors why they must focus on neurological health and brain balance to stay on the leading edge of the profession. His highly anticipated new book, *BrainTap, The Ultimate Guide to Relaxing, Rebooting and Strengthening Your Busy Brain* is due for release in 2016.

Dr. Porter has produced an arsenal of more than 650 audio-recorded motivational programs and creative visualization processes, and has sold more than 3 million books and recordings worldwide.

Got to: www.BrainTapTech.com

The Everlasting Truths

Paul Leendertse

What Do You Do, When You Don't Know, What You Don't Know

Fifteen years ago I was frustrated, afraid, and actually beginning to feel desperate for help. Desperate for a solution. Desperate for someone, anyone who knew how to help me—because I didn't. I was reaching a point where I would do just about anything to fix my pain. I was paying for University with my construction business, but had developed back pain. It had been getting progressively worse over a 2-year period, to the point where I could hardly work anymore. After a full week off of work to just rest—which I could not afford to do—my back pain still had not improved... I went to specialist after specialist and some of them provided relief but the pain would just come back. I even bought a new bed specifically to help relieve my back pain. If my back continued to get worse I was going to lose my business. What would I do about money?

I came across a book called, *How to Eat, Move and Be Healthy!* by Paul Chek, Founder of the Chek Institute, and read about gluten intolerance. I learned that back pain can be caused from eating gluten-containing grains, so I decided to stop eating gluten to see if it would help. What happened next was shocking and boy was I angry! Yes, I said angry! Let me explain! My back pain went away in four days—FOUR DAYS! I had back pain for over 2 years and probably accumulated a few grey hairs from all the constant stress associated with it! All it took was cutting specific grains out of my diet?! I came to realize that I simply had not known what I didn't know, and there's not much I could have done about my back pain without my new awareness.

It was so confusing because I had started eating "really healthy" around the same time I started my construction business, so I thought my work in construction had been hurting my back. But actually, I was making the choice to eat "X" servings of grains each day because that's what I believed was healthy. Today I know that I was following advice that really wasn't in alignment with what was truly good for *me*, hence, regardless of my strong desire to be healthy, my daily living reality was going against my health, rather than supporting it.

Something inside me changed forever. I came to a deep realization: *it was me who had been creating my back pain.* I had no idea how but I really had been creating my pain. I forgave myself for not knowing, I forgave anyone that tried to help but couldn't, and thanked Paul Chek for giving me back my power through the gift of awareness.

I also realized something else far more valuable. My body had no choice but actually create a pain signal as it responded to the "threat" (gluten) which was damaging my body. My body *had* to become inflamed, and *had* to send pain messages to let me know something was wrong. Something in my heart was truly awakened and I began a long, arduous journey investigating what else I did not know, that I did not know.

With this new epiphany, after graduating with an Honours Degree in Kinesiology from the University of Waterloo, I decided to pursue building my seasonal construction business with my wife Melissa. Each year I had four months of total freedom which provided me the opportunity to travel wherever needed in order to acquire awareness about health. I did a tremendous amount of research. I discovered that it isn't just physical things like food and exercise that affect our health—there are four realms that make up a human being and each affect our health! They are the physical, mental, emotional, and spiritual realms.

I interviewed many health experts and studied the teachings of health gurus, completed numerous certifications in holistic health and, *most importantly*, I went through significant personal transformations of personal growth in the physical (like my back), mental (thoughts), emotional (feelings) and spiritual (beliefs and personal responsibility) realms.

Years later a tragedy hit my family hard—my stepfather was diagnosed with lung cancer and he died. He died after using a huge regimen of both alternative and traditional approaches to combatting cancer. What made life worse was that only three months apart from my stepfather's diagnosis and death from cancer, my best friend's father also died of lung cancer, and he was a second father to me...

As a result of my experience with back pain I asked myself, "what if the body has no choice but create cancer for some unknown reason?" Something, after all, is missing in the main-stream understanding of and approach to preventing and healing cancer, considering the frightening reality of today that, statistically, 1 in every 2.2 people are developing cancer. With the question in my mind "could cancer cells have some kind of purpose in the body?" I went forward, passionate, and determined to somehow answer that question.

I invested over 15 years and easily more than $150,000 dollars learning everything I could about the physical, mental, emotional and spiritual realms that affect our health. I have read hundreds of books and research papers about health and in particular, cancer.

Eventually, I discovered a connection between sugar and cancer cells—it is a scientific fact that cancer cells absorb huge amounts of sugar out of our bloodstream. Excess sugar in our bloodstream is NOT healthy... and so I thought, "what if cancer cells are built by the body to absorb that sugar preventing the cellular damage that would otherwise occur?" But something was still missing. After all, sometimes people develop cancer and they have a healthy diet. I had almost dropped trying to figure out whether cancer cells could possibly have a purpose, and then an epiphany hit me...

I was sitting in a classroom in California completing a course in Holistic Health at the CHEK Institute, thinking about my stepfather who had died from lung cancer. In this particular class my instructor was teaching us about the fight-or-flight response and said something that grabbed my attention, she said, "when a person is stressed, the fight-or-flight response is triggered, which causes a huge surge of energy to help them fight or escape the perceived threat." When she said, "energy," my eyes widened and ears perked up so intensely I might have actually looked like a cat. I put my hand up and asked, "What do you mean by energy?" She said, "What are you trying to get at?" I asked, "When you say energy, do you mean sugar?" She thought about it and assumed after a brief moment, that yes, the medical literature is probably referring to sugar with regards to the effects of the fight-or-flight mechanism.

That's when the big AH-HA moment hit me! Cancer cells grow in response to chronic, excess blood sugar, that doesn't just surge from eating processed foods but also from *psychological stress!*

After three intensive years of research and writing, I wrote the *WHAT'S IN A TEAR?* 3-book series, beginning with book 1, *THE PURPOSE OF CANCER CELLS—Ten Everlasting Truth's That Can Change Your Life.*

A large amount of research supports without a doubt that cancer cells are a survival mechanism the body uses to extend a person's life. If we don't remove what's causing the blood sugar-surges (certain lifestyle factors and/or psychological stress, apparent or suppressed) then cancer cells can continue growing and become a major problem inside the body.

From five years of experience with cancer patients in my 1-Month Overcome Cancer Residency Program I have *discovered* and assembled Ten Everlasting Truths.

The Everlasting Truths are essential for mastering your life in all realms—the physical, mental, emotional, and spiritual, so that you can reach your true potential in health, happiness, and life-fulfillment, and prevent cancer. I want to share the Everlasting Truth's with you so that you significantly—and I mean significantly—increase your ability to heal if you've been diagnosed with cancer, or if you have less than optimal health.

By applying the Everlasting Truth's I've seen people heal themselves of psoriasis, lose 20lbs of excess weight, and have migraines disappear. I've seen women normally bed-ridden with painful menstrual cycles have absolutely no discomfort on their cycle once they started applying the Everlasting Truths. Painful hip, knee, and shoulder joints have experienced relief in a matter of days. I have even known men with erectile dysfunction experience a 'wake up!' , once they started incorporating the Everlasting Truths into their life. Yes, I've seen cancer lumps the size of a golf ball in the breast, abdomen, groin, or neck, disappear in a matter of weeks when these truths were applied. It does not matter what your unique health challenge might be or what your health, happiness, and goals of success are—applying The Everlasting Truths are the most essential building blocks.

There really does exist a set of rules, or "spiritual laws" that work every single time to support and maintain health and significantly increase a person's ability to heal from any disease. The result of the application of those laws (The Everlasting Truths) are actually permanent—your success with each one is everlasting. As an example, if you were to start drinking water each day, replacing other liquids, the water would benefit your well-being. Water does not one day stop benefiting you—you can always count on water!

The Everlasting Truths are not made up—they have existed forever (like water) and they support all human beings! They are sort of like the laws of physics here on Earth. Take for instance gravity: If you throw a stone up into the open sky it will come back down again every time—it is the law of gravity here on Earth. The law of gravity doesn't change and no one actually made that law—it was discovered. We can depend on the law of gravity and we do so in a myriad of ways. If that law were to change we'd be in trouble. If we did NOT respect or know of that law we'd also be in trouble! But no one or at least no human being we know of is in charge of that law—it just exists.

I want to share a few things with you to help increase your ability to be successful with the Everlasting Truth's:

Number 1: Each one of us has within us the ability to reach a high level of well-being, which means being successful, feeling happy, enjoying regular health, a loving relationship, and experiencing a vibrant, fulfilled state of being. If you have tried to achieve any of these and failed, I can assure you it's simply because you were not aware of the Everlasting Truths.

Number 2: The absolute importance of a holistic, open mind. A holistic mind means you are aware that everything and everyone is connected. Humans share a multitude of needs. If any of our needs are not met we will start declining in wholeness, and thus our health and vibrancy will diminish. For example, we all need to feel safe, breathe clean air, sleep well and drink clean water. If you were to stop sleeping, you would literally die, but on the flip side, the degree that you optimize your sleep, you thrive! The same holds true for water—you die without it and you thrive with the right amount of good clean water each day. These are four examples from the set of Everlasting Truths that when met in optimal ways, contribute to and elevate the degree of your well-being.

Let's think about the nature of the Everlasting Truths. We can literally die without them; *survive* if they are sub-optimally met; and thrive when they are adequately fulfilled! If we take a holistic view, we can see that if we remove any one of the Everlasting Truths our well-being is degraded because they are all connected. You can optimize water perfectly but if you aren't sleeping well you will still develop symptoms! They all serve us powerfully when we are aware of them and make them the foundation of our lives. One aspect of holistic thinking with regards to health means being aware that all humans share the same general *needs*, and they must be met in order to experience well-being. We are all very, very connected. The Everlasting Truths are all connected as well, each necessary to reach a complete degree of wholeness.

Next we need an open mind. An open mind means that you are open to the process of change. Often, an open mind requires having courage because the process of change can be truly scary! I'm not just referring to change around you—that matters but, I'm referring more to a change that can occur within you. In the process of growing awareness the most important thing to be open to is the changing of beliefs about what is good versus bad in any aspect of our lives. Beliefs are often deeply intertwined with fears such as, "that's impossible!" or "I can't." The truth as goal you sincerely want to set is possible, and you can! Things just take time to change!

Now I'd like to introduce you to the Ten Everlasting Truth Categories!

The Ten Everlasting Truth's:

1. Physical needs
2. Needs of the natural world
3. The need for goals
4. The need for mind mastery
5. Emotional needs
6. Communication needs
7. The need for virtues
8. The need for play
9. Spiritual needs
10. The need for self-love.

If you are experiencing negative symptoms in your body, are unhappy, or have developed cancer, I honestly believe the only way to truly reverse these symptoms and create long-term health and happiness, is by filling in any missing links within the Everlasting Truth's. Here are the Everlasting Truth's subcategories:

1. Physical needs
   - Nutrition
   - Hydration
   - Rest
   - Oxygen
   - Movement
2. Needs of the natural world
   - Connection to Earth
   - Connection to Sun
   - Connection to Water
   - Connection to Air
   - Connection to Nature
3. The need for goals
   - Motivation
   - Expansion
   - Focus
4. The need for mind mastery
   - Effective thinking in the past
   - No mind (not thinking)
   - Effective thinking in the future
5. Emotional needs
   - Feeling safe
   - Connection to self and others

- Personal power - freedom, self-esteem, confidence
6. Communication needs
   - Connective listening
   - Connective expressing
7. The need for virtues
   - Creating good karma
   - Using virtues wisely
8. The need for unbound play. One or more forms of:
   - spontaneous art
   - spontaneous dance
   - spontaneous music
   - spontaneous crafts
   - spontaneous adventure
   - spontaneous play
9. Spiritual needs
   - Meaningful life path (Legacy)
   - Personal responsibility
   - Letting go of beliefs
10. The need for self-love.
   - Self-love
   - Sharing love
   - Giving and receiving love

The WHAT'S IN A TEAR? Series gives you the opportunity to know and embody each of these categories so that you can strengthen your ability to prevent cancer or overcome cancer, and accomplish optimal health and happiness.

What could be beneficial for you right now is to look at the ELT list and ask yourself which categories you are adequately addressing or feel healthy and whole about. Then, ask yourself which ones you likely need to work on —ones are likely related to stress in your life due to their need for fulfillment.

Using the Everlasting Truth's is like putting a puzzle together. If pieces of puzzle are missing, the puzzle is not yet whole. If a person has any kind of health or happiness challenge the reason is a missing puzzle piece—an Everlasting Truth category that needs to be remedied or fulfilled.

All of the Everlasting Truths are aspects of life that we need, yet they don't have to be perfected. We simply need to engage in the process of striving towards improvement in areas that may be lacking. This keeps us growing into our future in healthy ways. To the degree that we optimize each of the Truth's our life shapes into one that keeps us inspired, energized, and eager to get out of bed in the morning! Addressing them and applying them is a rewarding process, and can be challenging as the process often means "waking up" to what we didn't know. But the process is empowering and life-serving!

Here is a basic example from a case history of a client I've worked with, of how the Everlasting Truth's can be applied to basically any health challenge. Even the simplest of the Everlasting Truths are essential for long-term health and healing:

Everlasting Truth#1, PHYSICAL NEEDS: Water

I had a client once who came to me with a bad knee, whose goal was to lose weight. Prior to this she had been working out with a trainer in the gym three days a week, kicking butt! However, after two years of making progress losing weight and increasing her fitness level she ended up developing a painful knee, and had to stop exercising altogether. In a very short period of time she gained all her weight back *and more.*

When I looked at her overall approach to her goals she was missing several of Everlasting Truths—one example was water. One of the facts about water is that we each need to drink about ½ our body weight in ounces of water per day. Water is crucial for the health of every cell in our body. For example, it is a scientific fact that water is the main ingredient in synovial fluid—the main lubricant for the joints in our body. The human being is like a vehicle in some ways—it has moving parts that need to be lubricated. Water is far more important than this though—it is a requirement for the healthy functioning of all organs and all systems of the body! Every single cell in our body is made out of 70% or more of water! Imagine what would happen if you stopped putting oil in your engine and continued to drive your vehicle? To heal her knee and get back into exercise, she started drinking enough water each day along with addressing the other missing elements of the Everlasting Truth's. She no longer has any issue with her knee.

There is something very special about each of the Everlasting Truths that is the reason behind why they are so powerful. The reason is love—a scientifically immeasurable phenomenon.

Love is in water...isn't it? Let me ask you a question: Is clean water nourishing for some but not others? Does drinking clean water ever damage us? Do you see the love within water? Love is also in whole organic food and free-range, lovingly raised animals. It's why these foods create and sustain optimal health but processed foods or sick, unhappy animals do not... Unfortunately, many scientific studies done with regards to the question of whether eating meat is healthy or not are done on unhealthy, unhappy animals. Only free-range, lovingly raised animals should ever be consumed with the goal of a having an ongoing, high level of well-being.

Love is in sleep and it is one of the most powerful physical sources of healing and regeneration there is, and it's free! Love is in healthy movement because motion pumps your body fluids, keeps you strong, and allows you to walk towards your dreams. Love is in clean air because it nourishes every single cell in your body when you breathe it and every other living being as well! Love is in positive thoughts and emotions and only these ones create and maintain wholeness. Love is in healthy freedom which is why you must follow your heart! Last but not least, love is always best for all. Love is the main ingredient in every single one of the Everlasting Truths!

The inherent quality of the Everlasting Truth's is that each of us has the ability to work towards and accomplish higher and higher levels of their embodiment—they are within the reach of everyone who sets goals to achieve them! Without exception, anyone who focuses on them moves closer and closer to bodymind wholeness. Thank you for being part of the "wake up!" process —I wish you success through you entire journey! I hope I have connected you to at least one thing that will help you in your life-goals, something that maybe you did not know, you did not know!

About the Author

Paul Leendertse

Founder of *The Transcend Cancer Movement.* C.H.E.K Practitioner & CHEK

Holistic Lifestyle Coach

Former Certified Kinesiologist

Personal, Professional, Spiritual, Success Mastery (ppssuccess.com)

Creator of *Wheel of Life*:
1. Healing Through Cancer Residency Program.
2. Body, Mind, and Soul Mastery Courses.
3. Cancer Prevention Mastery Course.

Author of the What's in a Tear? Cancer Book Series
Book 1: The Purpose of Cancer: *The One Thing That the War on Cancer Has Been Missing, Since the Beginning, That Makes the Difference.*
Book 2: Transcending Cancer: *Freedom from Inner and Outer War*
Book 3: The End of Cancer: *Transcending Cancer by Transforming Our Lives*

www.thepurposeofcancer.com

Wired to be W'healthy!

Rick Glade

There is an overwhelming thought running through 90% or more of all the people I meet. By the time I get involved in helping them create a life by design instead of living one by default, it's always the questions of: Have I wasted too much of my life? Is there enough time left for me to make a difference? Do I have what it takes to become W'healthy?

The short answer is you are never too young or old to start living and sharing a vibrant lifestyle. Your life is what you make of it. It's your choice to become as healthy or wealthy as you choose. You can rewire or begin wiring your brain for absolute health and wealth, but is has to be in that order. Health first, wealth second. Most people get it backwards; they sacrifice health and longevity to achieve wealth without ever being conscious of it.

Ask yourself this question: If you had $10 million or even $10 million in Bitcoin crypto currency, but only had 10 minutes to live, the money doesn't do a whole lot of good. You must realize that health consciousness is an equal or greater part of success.

When I was younger, I thought I was invincible. I wasn't born being fed from a silver spoon. However, I decided I would create my own set of utensils to feed my mind and own my own luck! I had to reprogram the software of my mind to be W'healthy. You see, most people walk across the stages of life and realize they have never created anything by design, but simply lived a life by default, day in and day out. Ask yourself if you are intentionally making the right mental and physical choices for a sustainable path to a vibrant lifestyle. Before you answer this, let me first congratulate you on your all your accomplishments! Some have accomplished more or less than others. Whether big or small, you are where you are.

I want to assure you that my message is only one of awareness. I want nothing more than your real life journey to begin from today. You are now one of us. The purpose of this book is to share chapter-by-chapter how we all have gained individual vibrant lifestyles through several modalities, some with a common thread. From this day forward, maybe nothing will seem familiar to you. Maybe you have already begun your journey. Whichever it is, choosing to live a vibrant future will be the most rewarding experience ever! This next phase of your journey is entirely up to you, and your success will be determined by the choices you make.

You may be asking yourself, *how do I get to be W'healthy?*

We are all individuals with different personalities, aspirations, and skill sets. These are shaped and develop over time based on our experiences, beliefs, and environment. This is where living in a state of mental and physical awareness is most beneficial, and it took me a long time to master this skill. All of us are capable of reprogramming our minds to accept things in one of two ways: positive or negative and fearful or fearless. It is all based on our perception. I want to say that fear is normal and real; in fact, it's a natural part of our anatomy and the fight-or-flight rule that is hardwired into our autonomic nervous system. Perception, however, is an entirely conscious choice.

Think of the very first time you rode a bicycle. Your mind and body was riddled with fear, the what ifs, and fear of the unknown. But as you gained momentum and confidence, it became second nature and now your brain is hardwired for life. It now has taken on what we refer to as muscle memory. You will never fear mounting a bicycle again. This same type of muscle memory can be hardwired in to any aspect of your life.

I want to share with you a concept of living in the moment. Literally! Shut down your reactions to the little voice inside your head. I can assure you if the voice inside your head had the answers to what happens next, it would have already revealed itself. The reality is the answer has to appear in the moment... in the NOW. That is how clarity to all questions you have will be answered. This is the first step to clearing your mind of jargon: by focusing on the present moment. I knew that pausing or living in the NOW wasn't something I felt I was programmed to do. Honestly, I didn't even know if I could actually do that. It was the best thing I have ever implemented into my life.

I know right now that everybody asks the same questions: How is living in the now going to stop my fear or improve my life? (Because I know your mind is going a hundred miles an hour with thoughts and self-talk...so many questions and thoughts spinning inside your head.) And here you are, sitting there ready to hit the fast-forward button and find out the answers. I get that. I was just LIKE you: I lived on fast-forward. Before you go ahead and press that button, I hope you'll take this advice and have the fortitude to first press the pause button. That's right: Even better yet, press the stop button. I hope if you learn anything from me, you learn and remember the power of *right now!*

Yes, the questions in your head are real, and the question of "What happens next?" follows us our whole lives. It comes in many forms, but it's always there. No matter what you do or how much you accomplish, the chatter in our minds will constantly rattle thought after thought. The past is gone forever. If you are living in the past, you are either depressed or angry. If you are living in the future, you are anxious or stressed. The answers will reveal themselves in due time. Be patient.

So at a time when people are overwhelmed by the thought of what their next meal choice will be, let alone the next phase of their life, PAUSE. Live in the moment and take the time to find out what's important to you. Find out what you love to do and who do you love to do it for. What are your true core values that make you take action?

I want to make sure I'm clear here. I am not suggesting you

ignore planning for the future. Rather, I am merely saying the future will change moment by moment from what you might have assumed or predicted it would be. You will have to accept that new reality from what you perceived it was going to be. Let me give you some extreme examples to make my point. Have you ever seen a weather person predict the wrong forecast? Have you ever made travel plans that changed instantly due to factors outside of your control? Have you ever been caught in a power outage? Have you ever been laid off or fired? The point is that you had no idea your present moment would turn out differently than you originally planned. You must be agile enough to embrace it.

I will tell you two truths I know to be fact. You will never earn your way to financial freedom. You either have to invest your way there or create it on your own. What do I mean by that? It means you will have to use your current resources as a vehicle to invest your way to wealth by using those earnings to acquire assets that pay you back in cash flow without you having to go to work. Alternatively, create a business or venture that you can sell for a profitable liquidity event far above your basis in that business to create wealth in the future. The latter is harder and generally more work.

As you move into what must seem like an uncertain future, let me share with you the 10 W'healthy principles of wisdom I wish I knew early on:

1. Have a plan—but accept change often. We have all been taught to have a plan. Go to this school, achieve certain grades, pick a certain major. And when you graduate, get a job, make your salary, get promoted, and work your way up the ladder. I call BS because hardly anything ever works according to plan.

While having a plan is good for providing structure and focus, life never seems to go accordingly. There are always twists and turns; and a plan never accounts for how you evolve and change as you move throughout your journey. Instead, have a plan but use it as a rough roadmap. Understand that any plan is a reflection of what you think your journey is at a particular moment in time and be prepared to change it radically and often.

2. Be the most authentic version of yourself—all the time. If you want to be an actor, go to Hollywood. For everyone else, be who you really are.

You may bring different parts of personality or strengths with you to your career choice other than you do at home with your family and friends, but you should be your real self all the time. Figure out what is important to you and who you want to be in the world, and live that as honestly as you can. Your authenticity must shine through. Your social network will evolve to equal your net worth.

3. Your first job should be about experience. The first jobs are not always the highest-paying jobs or at the best companies. Your first job should provide the opportunity to work with people you can learn from, where you receive on-the-job training, and gain a set of basic skills, where there is the opportunity for you to develop and grow, and where success means improving your personal brand! Always be growing.

4. In the beginning, forget work-life balance. If you want to work with great people, solve tough problems, and leave the world better off because of your work, it's tough to have work-life balance. If you want to invent a new technology or discover a cure for a disease, it is all-consuming. I'm not saying that you can't go to yoga, play sports, or have a social and family life; but, for certain periods of your life, you should plan to be out of that balance. Not only will you recognize true life balance when it comes, but you will be most grateful for it as well. However, remember to always strive for whatever balances you, too. Don't forget to live along the way. People are always more important than things!

5. There are no shortcuts. There is no fast lane to success. People who think so usually don't have it for long. Work hard to master something or create circumstances to be successful; work in the right environment, build the right relationships, and remain open to new opportunities to develop and grow. Remember life is not fair, not everybody gets a trophy, and there will be times of setbacks. These hiccups will evolve to your biggest strides of accomplishment.

6. Take calculated risks. So many of you will choose to play it safe by doing what the masses do. But if you are presented with an opportunity to step out of your comfort zone and take a measured risk—a job that is a stretch or investing in opportunities you may not know much about, don't dismiss it outright. Instead, ask yourself: what are the risks versus rewards, will I learn, and if it's a complete failure, will I survive? Never risk more than you can afford to lose without having to start over!

7. Have great mentors. There is nothing more impactful on your journey to becoming W'healthy and personal development than having great mentors—people who have experience in what you're seeking and are willing to guide you, provide you with real feedback, and help you grow. Find a mentor and openly engage with him or her. I've been fortunate to have a few really great mentors in my life and know that I would not have been able to develop into the person that I am without their influence.

8. Be the kind of person everyone wants at their side. Be the person who leans in and adds value to every equation. Be the creative, thoughtful, assertive, natural leader who functions well in team situations. This type of person is humble but has just enough ego that they can't fail.

9. Follow your passion. Write your own script and own your own luck! Experience life fully, find out the things that drive you, immerse yourself in it and, above all, work on things that you are passionate about. To be truly engaged and ultimately be successful—however you define success—you must engage both your head and heart. If you can create a lifestyle built on passion, your chances for success, fulfillment, and longevity are far greater.

10. Be grateful. This final one is about how you carry yourself and your perspective mindset. It is the foundation of all W'healthy people. You are among the luckiest in our society. You have the present and the world is, in fact, your oyster. As you make your way through life, pay it forward for people—both literally and figuratively. As full of promise your future is, you will learn that being fluent in kindness goes a long way.

As you take this jump into the deep end, take a look back at what you have accomplished so far and be proud and grateful. Be thankful to those who helped you get here. Look to the future with an open heart and open mind. Finally, as you move into your future, do so with passion, love, and the pursuit of mastery. Be W'healthy!

We all need to get to a place of being content with our lives. I haven't met a single person who doesn't still feel overwhelmed at times by the "So, now what?" Question. We all will experience the unknown for the rest of our lives; sadly, it is endless. I want to remind you can hit the pause button and enjoy living in the moment!

I hope that by reading or listening to this chapter, I have brought some awareness and guidance for the road that lies ahead. Don't worry if you don't have all of the answers right away. They will come in the now, so be patient and enjoy the journey.

Remember, this life is all about the eulogy and not the resume; nobody will care about what degrees you hold or how many initials you have behind your name. It won't matter much what you've accumulated along the way, like how many cars or homes you own. They will remember you for the love and the wisdom and legacy you left behind. They will remember the contribution and the lives you touched.

With all my intention, I wish you the best of living a W'healthy and vibrant life filled with sustainable success!

About the Author

Rick Glade

I would appreciate if you found value in my chapter to reach out to me at www.realwealthwhisperer.com or www.infinitesuccessalliance.com and send me a message directly.

WAKE UP INC—RESOURCES PAGE

Would you like to write your own book?

We do all types of books. Hardback/paperback books - ebooks - audio books - children's books - novels - self-help - business books.

Let # 1 book coach Steven E. Schmitt and his team of over 20 professional editors, cover and book designers help you.

We also help with marketing and making bestsellers on Amazon. com and New York Times bestsellers. See bestsellerguru.com

We make it easy for you:—

See Steven E. Schmitt's YouTube channel with over 100 book marketing videos.

Do you have a story ?

Go to wakeuplive,com and see if you have a story for our up and coming Wake Up books.

Go to YouTube.com and search bestsellerguru for 100 videos.

Or email: Selawofpositivity@gmail.com

Tel: (562) 884 0062

CPSIA information can be obtained
at www.ICGtesting.com
Printed in the USA
FSHW020755300720